T0233346

Android Continuous Integration

Build-Deploy-Test Automation for Android Mobile Apps

Pradeep Macharla

Apress®

Android Continuous Integration

Pradeep Macharla
North Carolina, USA

ISBN-13 (pbk): 978-1-4842-2795-4   ISBN-13 (electronic): 978-1-4842-2796-1
DOI 10.1007/978-1-4842-2796-1

Library of Congress Control Number: 2017953099

Cover image designed by Freepik

Managing Director: Welmoed Spahr
Editorial Director: Todd Green
Acquisitions Editor: Nikhil Karkal
Development Editor: Matthew Moodie
Technical Reviewer: Ankita Gupta
Coordinating Editor: Prachi Mehta
Copy Editor: Kezia Endsley
Compositor: SPi Global
Indexer: SPi Global
Artist: SPi Global

Distributed to the book trade worldwide by Springer Science+Business Media New York, 233 Spring Street, 6th Floor, New York, NY 10013. Phone 1-800-SPRINGER, fax (201) 348-4505, e-mail orders-ny@springer-sbm.com, or visit www.springeronline.com. Apress Media, LLC is a California LLC and the sole member (owner) is Springer Science + Business Media Finance Inc (SSBM Finance Inc). SSBM Finance Inc is a **Delaware** corporation.

For information on translations, please e-mail rights@apress.com, or visit http://www.apress.com/rights-permissions.

Apress titles may be purchased in bulk for academic, corporate, or promotional use. eBook versions and licenses are also available for most titles. For more information, reference our Print and eBook Bulk Sales web page at http://www.apress.com/bulk-sales.

Any source code or other supplementary material referenced by the author in this book is available to readers on GitHub via the book's product page, located at www.apress.com/978-1-4842-2795-4. For more detailed information, please visit http://www.apress.com/source-code.

Printed on acid-free paper

This book is dedicated to all the software engineers who are passionate about coding and feel the urgency to fix that which is broken, spend odd hours at night deeply involved in solving the problem, derive gratification when it works, yet repeat it all over when it doesn't the next day. To all who ultimately appreciate the fact that software is art and singularity is the future.

Contents at a Glance

Contents

About the Author

Pradeep Macharla is a passionate technical and business leader managing, coaching and growing teams around the globe ranging from Fortune 500 to small and medium companies. His background and experience has made him a highly sought after technical coach and mentor, consulting or working at the senior leadership and executive level with companies spanning across industries where Digital and IT technologies have significant impact. Pradeep has been an integral part of several initiatives in the technology space including mobile, web, financial and consulting services. His github provides an insight into domains of interest. Pradeep likes to play table tennis for stress busting.

About the Technical Reviewer

Ankita Gupta is a software test professional with experience in automation for web and mobile, and security and performance testing. She has a background of working with companies including PayPal, LinkedIn, Airtel, Wingify, and Expedia. Ankita has previously spoken at NullCon, NewGen Testing Conf., and Selenium Conf. She has also contributed to open source projects related to web-based automation.

Acknowledgments

While technology constantly changes, the need to optimize, accelerate, and see things from newer perspectives is a fundamental human need. I owe my learning and inspiration to the open source community on StackOverflow, GitHub, and countless blogs, including the Appium web site. I also want to thank the Apress team (Nikhil, Matt, and Prachi) for grooming the book to a presentable state and collaborating patiently.

CHAPTER 1

Introduction

This chapter sets the context and the current mobile landscape. We start by introducing the overall architectural pattern and the definition of Continuous Integration (CI) and subsequently list the installation steps of the tools and software that form the platform. The underlying software platform (Jenkins, Nexus, SonarQube, and Docker, et al.) form the foundation on which we build automation concepts.

Architecture

In this book, I present a pattern for *CI*,a.k.a. quick feedback as soon as the developer checks in the code. Although the term CI for some involves merging and building code in a distributed model, in this book, you will not only merge code, but also build, deploy, and test it. Only when you complete the loop of build-deploy-test (the key piece is testing) will you be confident about the quality of the code you checked in.

You will start with a minimum viable product (*MVP)* that follows the architecture shown in Figure 1-1. All steps in the process are completely automated—no exceptions!

© Pradeep Macharla 2017
P. Macharla, *Android Continuous Integration*, DOI 10.1007/978-1-4842-2796-1_1

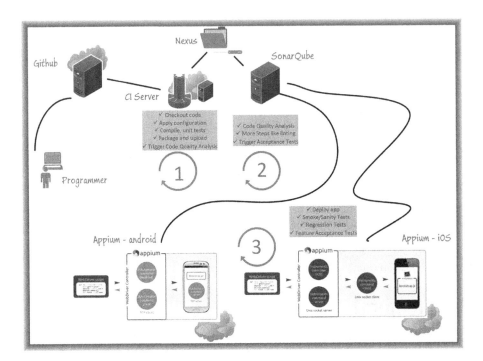

Figure 1-1. *Overall architecture*

As you reach initial maturity with the CI feedback loop and see continuous builds and feedback, you will continue to push the envelope and achieve parallel device testing. Figure 1-2 shows the Test Runner architecture.

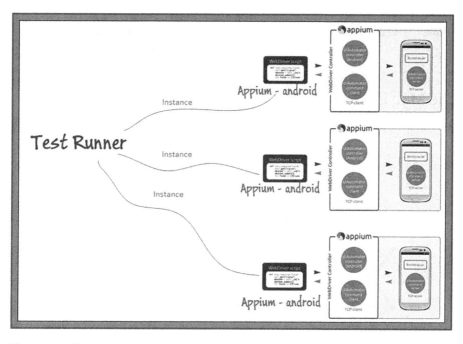

Figure 1-2. *Test Runner architecture*

Prerequisites

The following sections cover the software tools needed to follow the code patterns in this book.

Windows vs. Mac

To develop an Android app, you can use either Mac or Windows platforms. However, I recommend using Mac over Windows because of the following experiences I had:

- Device drivers are easier to obtain on a Mac (as opposed to Windows, where you have to identify the hardware and go to the vendor's web site)

- System resources (CPU, RAM, etc.) perform better on a Mac

- The emulator performs relatively better on a Mac

- Most online examples refer to the Mac environment

- Android OS is a *nix core underneath, hence the experience of developing, debugging, and testing feels better on a Mac

---

■ **Note**   This book uses a Mac for the hardware and for the underlying OS.

The Mac Environment

The Mac environment shown in Figure 1-3 was used to run all the examples in this book.

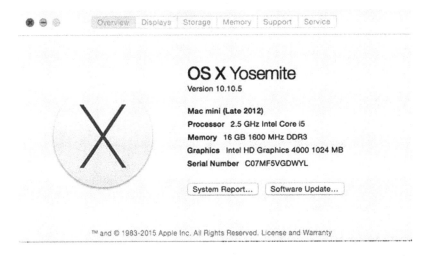

Figure 1-3. *Mac environment used for the book's examples*

Mobile Devices

You should have at least one real Android device. It's best to have an Android 4.4 operating system or above, API 17 or above. With Android 4.2 and earlier, the appium server needs to be started with selendroid-port in addition to bootstrap-port. Details of port values are listed in Chapter 8, "Work with Appium".

Network

It's best if all the servers (Jenkins, Nexus, Sonar, Appium, etc.) and the build machine were in the same network segment. At a minimum, they should be able to ping (assuming ICMP is not disabled) and be able to reach each other on the ports that the processes listen (mostly TCP). (For example, if Jenkins were running on web 8080, you should be able to reach http://jenkins_url:8080 from all other machines.)

Platform

The following domain knowledge is required to a certain extent.

- Java programming language and runtime (the Android app source is in Java)

- Ruby programming language (understand the automation framework written with Cucumber and Ruby)

- Usage of *nix operating systems (the Mac aligns with *nix style)

Programming Language

The test automation framework uses the Ruby programming language. I chose Ruby with Gherkin, since it's close to reading the English language.

Installation Processes

For each software program you need, the installation instructions are provided. At the end of each section, you'll find a link to a video demonstrating the installation process.

Installing Jenkins

The version of Jenkins installed at the time of writing this book is 1.642.1.
Use the following steps to install Jenkins:

1. Log in to a machine that has Docker installed on it (installation instructions for Docker, which are machine dependent, are found at https://docs.docker.com/engine/installation/). This example uses Ubuntu 14.04 OS.

2. Run the command docker run -d -name "myjenkins" -p 8083:8080 jenkins:*latest* (latest at the time of this writing is the 1.642.1 version of Jenkins).

3. Access the Jenkins URL using http://hostname:8083.

4. Navigate to Manage Jenkins ➤ Manager Users. Add a user with the name admin and provide a password.

5. Navigate to Manage Jenkins ➤ Configure Global Security. Check the Enable Security checkbox. On the same page, under Access Control, select Jenkin's Own User Database. Under Authorization, select Matrix-Based Security.

6. Add a user called admin and check all the boxes in all the columns (for more detailed instructions, watch the video).

7. Now save the page. This will focus the page to the user login.

8. Log in as the `admin` user.

9. Click New Item in the left menu, provide an Item Name of `HelloWorld`, and click OK.

10. Go to Build ➤ Add Build Step ➤ Execute Shell.

11. In the text area, type `echo "hello world"` and click Save.

12. Click Build Now in the left menu.

13. The build passes in and a blue ball shows up against the entry in Build History.

14. If you want to see the console output, click the build number (#1) and then click Console Output.

Jenkins is successfully installed now. Figure 1-4 shows the UI.

Figure 1-4. *Jenkins UI*

The link to the video demonstrating the steps is `https://vimeo.com/154497273`.

Installing Nexus

The version of Nexus installed at the time of writing this book is 2.11.4-01. Use the following steps to install Nexus:

1. Log in to your machine that has Docker installed on it (installation instructions for Docker, which are machine dependent, are found at `https://docs.docker.com/engine/installation/`). This example uses Ubuntu 14.04 OS.

2. Run the command `docker run -d -name "mynexus" -p 8081:8081 sonatype/nexus:oss` (the latest at the time of this writing is 2.11.4-01).

3. Access the Nexus URL using `http://localhost:8081` (the default credentials are `admin/admin123`).

Nexus is successfully installed now, and the UI is shown in Figure 1-5.

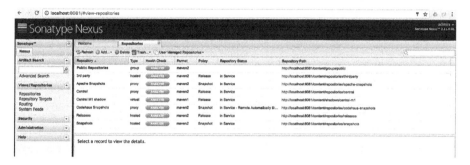

Figure 1-5. *Nexus UI*

Check out `https://vimeo.com/154500108` to see how to install Nexus.

Installing SonarQube

The version of SonarQube installed at the time of writing this book is 5.1. Use the following steps to install SonarQube:

1. Log in to your machine that has Docker installed on it (installation instructions for Docker, which are machine dependent, are found at `https://docs.docker.com/engine/installation/`). This example uses Ubuntu 14.04 OS.

2. Run the command `docker run -d -name "mysonarqube" -p 9000:9000 sonarqube:5.1` (the latest version at the time of writing is 5.1).

3. Access the SonarQube URL using `http://localhost:9000` (the default credentials are `admin/admin`).

SonarQube is successfully installed now, and its UI is shown in Figure 1-6.

Figure 1-6. *SonarQube UI*

Check out `https://vimeo.com/154499186` to see how to install SonarQube.

Installing the CI Tool Stack

Until now, you have installed the tools individually; however, there is another option to install all of them at once (if you prefer). This section is optional.

1. Log in to your machine that has Docker installed on it (installation instructions for Docker, which are machine dependent, are found at `https://docs.docker.com/engine/installation/`). This example uses Ubuntu 14.04 OS. Alternately, you can have `docker-machine` do all the work for you.

2. Use the check out code `git clone https://github.com/machzqcq/docker-ci-tool-stack.git`.

3. Run `docker-compose` up from the root of the folder.

The table of tools listed in Figure 1-7 will be ready in a few seconds (not more than 60 seconds).

Tool	Link	Credentials
Jenkins	http://${docker-machine ip default}:18080/	no login required
SonarQube	http://${docker-machine ip default}:19000/	admin/admin
Nexus	http://${docker-machine ip default}:18081/nexus	admin/admin123
GitLab	http://${docker-machine ip default}:10080/	root/5iveL!fe
Selenium Grid	http://${docker-machine ip default}:4444/grid/console	no login required

Figure 1-7. *CI tool stack endpoints*

Check out `https://vimeo.com/154935657` to see how to install the CI tool stack.

Building the Android App

The build-deploy-test feedback loop starts with the *build* process. The video at
`https://vimeo.com/154936765` quickly walks through the steps involved in building
an Android app. The Android app you are building here is only for demonstrating how
to build an app. In later chapters, when you get to test automation, you will start from
the source code and walk through detailed steps to reach the build phase.

■ **Note**   Watching the video is *not* mandatory to move forward in the book, but it gives you
a fast-forward view of the value-add from this book. You may conveniently skip this video
and come back after completing the book. Chapter 5, "Build Android App," has detailed
instructions and steps if you prefer text instructions.

Check out `https://vimeo.com/154936765` to see how to install the Android app.

Deploying/Installing the Android App

The *deploy* step in build-deploy-test is when the app becomes real and available to
interact. The video quickly walks through the steps involved in building an Android app.
The Android app you are deploying here is only for demonstrating how to build an app.
In later chapters, when you get to test automation, you will start from the source code and
walk through detailed steps to reach the deploy phase.

■ **Note**   Watching the video is *not* mandatory to move forward in the book, but it gives you
a fast-forward view of the value-add from this book. You may conveniently skip this video
and come back after completing the book. Chapter 7, "Deploy or Install Android App," has
detailed instructions and steps if you prefer text instructions.

Check out `https://vimeo.com/155159581` to see how to deploy the Android app.

Testing (Automating) the Android App

The *test* step in the build-deploy-test feedback loop tells you whether the app meets the
specifications and requirements. The test phase feedback is passed into the developer's
queue to improvise and/or fix bugs. The video fast-forwards the end-state solution when
running the automated tests against the app.

■ **Note** Watching the video is *not* mandatory to move forward in the book, but it gives you a fast-forward view of the value-add from this book. You may conveniently skip this video and come back after completing the book. Chapter 8, "Working to Appium," and Chapter 9, "Test Strategy and Execution," include detailed instructions and steps if you prefer text instructions.

Check out `https://www.youtube.com/watch?v=In9sCFrv-D0&feature=youtu.be` to see how to test the Android app.

Mobile Technologies

Mobile involves hardware, software, platforms, apps, and the overall experience. You can also look at smart vs. other mobile devices. To put perspective on mobile technologies, some attributes that help filter the avalanche of information are listed next.

What Do Consumers Want?

See `https://info.dynatrace.com/rs/compuware/images/Mobile_App_Survey_Report.pdf` for a great read from Dynatrace.

Ecosystems

Much like how Microsoft, Redhat, Canonical, et al. represent ecosystems in the operating systems space, there are ecosystems that are present in the mobile apps domain too. Ecosystems are entry points into the platforms on which mobile applications are developed, maintained, delivered, and enhanced.

At the time of writing this book, the ecosystems are broadly classified into the following categories.

- Apple
- Google
- Windows

Within each ecosystem, there can be many more categories, especially in the Google Android ecosystem (based on phone manufacturer, such as Huawei), as it provides more flexibility than Apple to tinker with the hardware architecture.

Hardware

Here is a sampling of the hardware you will encounter when developing mobile apps:

- Apple
- Samsung
- Sony
- HTC
- Qualcom
- Motorola
- Huawei
- Lenovo
- LG

You can read more at https://en.wikipedia.org/wiki/List_of_best-selling_mobile_phones.

Platforms/OS

The four main platforms are:

- iOS
- Android
- Windows
- Firefox OS

Types of Mobile Apps

There are different types of mobile apps that meet various needs. The decision on the type of mobile app is based on multiple factors. Here are the types that exist at the time of writing this book (see Figure 1-8).

- **Native apps**: Mobile apps that are entirely developed using the tool stack available in the respective ecosystem (Apple, Google, Windows, etc.) are called native apps. The tool stack could mean the programming language, the SDK, the underlying platform, and so on. Native apps by far give the best user experience and performance.

- **Web apps/HTML5 apps**: Apps that use web technologies like HTML5, JavaScript, and CSS that align with w3c standards are called web apps. Web apps do not heavily rely on native platform support and hence are more cross-platform and portable. That said, there is significant opportunity for improvement in the areas of secure local storage and access to device functionalities, like accelerometers, scanners, cameras, etc.

- **Hybrid apps**: Hybrid, as the name suggests, takes the positives of both web and native apps and brings them together.

NATIVE vs. WEB vs. HYBRID: **7 FACTORS OF COMPARISON**			KEY: CON PRO NEUTRAL
	NATIVE	HYBRID	WEB
COST	Commonly the highest of the three choices if developing for multiple platforms	Similar to pure web costs, but extra skills are required for hybrid tools	Lowest cost due to single codebase and common skillset
CODE REUSABILITY/	Code for one platform only works for that platform	Most hybrid tools will enable portability of a single codebase to the major mobile platforms	Browser compatiblity and performance are the only concerns
DEVICE ACCESS	Platform SDK enables access to all device APIs	Many device APIs closed to web apps can be accessed, depending on the tools	Only a few device APIs like the geolocation can be accessed, but the number is growing
UI CONSISTENCY	Platform comes with familiar, original UI components	UI frameworks can achieve a fairly native look	UI frameworks can achieve a fairly native look
DISTRIBUTION	App stores provide marketing benefits, but also have requirements and restrictions	App stores provide marketing benefits, but also have requirements and restrictions	No restrictions to launch, but there are no app store benefits
PERFORMANCE	Native code has direct access to platform functionality, resulting in better performance	For complex apps, the abstraction layers often prevent native-like performance	Performance is based on browser and network connection
MONETIZATION	More monetization opportunities, but stores take a percentage	More monetization opportunities, but stores take a percentage	No store commissions or setup costs, but there are few monetization methods

Figure 1-8. *Comparing mobile app types*

You can read more at https://dzone.com/articles/state-native-vs-web-vs-hybrid. This book covers native Android mobile apps.

CHAPTER 2

■ ■ ■

Mobile Test Automation

This chapter makes a case for mobile test automation and why it makes sense to invest in automation from the onset of your mobile app development process. The chapter also compares and contrasts the benefits of automation over manual testing practices. But first, you'll learn about a few evolutionary concepts, some of which are borrowed from web application test automation.

The WebDriver Protocol

WebDriver is a remote control interface that enables introspection and control of user agents. It provides a platform and language-neutral wire protocol as a way for out-of-process programs to remotely instruct the behavior of web browsers. A brief processing model is explained.

The *remote end* (see `https://www.w3.org/TR/webdriver/#dfn-remote-end`) is an HTTP server reading requests from the client and writing responses, typically over a TCP socket. For the purposes of this discussion, I model the data transmission between a particular local end and remote end with a connection to which the remote end may write and read bytes.

After such a connection has been established, a remote end must run the following steps:

1. Read bytes from the connection until an HTTP request can be constructed from the data.

2. The HTTP request is matched with the request's method and URL as parameters.

3. If the request match is of type `error`, send an error and error code, then return to Step 1.

4. Let the session ID be the corresponding variable from the URL variables.

© Pradeep Macharla 2017   13
P. Macharla, *Android Continuous Integration*, DOI 10.1007/978-1-4842-2796-1_2

5. If the command is New Session (and doesn't match the existing session's ID), then go back to Step 1.

6. Execute the request and collect the response object.

7. Send the response code and the results to the local end and return to Step 1.

For further details on WebDriver Protocol, see https://w3c.github.io/webdriver/webdriver-spec.html.

Selenium, the popular web test automation software, is based on the WebDriver protocol as its base layer. In fact, as you progress in the book, you will notice that the Appium communication also follows the WebDriver protocol.

Why Are We Talking About These Protocols?

Much like how micro-service APIs over monolithic applications are preferred in distributed systems, to take advantage of horizontal scaling, a similar innovation has happened in the past decade. Selenium (see https://en.wikipedia.org/wiki/Selenium_(software), with its relatively lightweight architecture, is fast replacing many licensed and enterprise tools.

There are web sites that have covered the web test automation use cases at http://www.seleniumframework.com/.

Many mobile automation tools and frameworks adopt principles of web test automation tools. That means that understanding the history of web test automation tools helps you connect the evolution tools like Appium, Calabash, and other open source mobile automation tools.

How Does It Work?

The client library (the test automation scripts) communicates with an intermediary server, which in turn translates into commands understood by the browser. This eventually emulates an end user's actions on the browser (actually it operates on the DOM). See Figure 2-1.

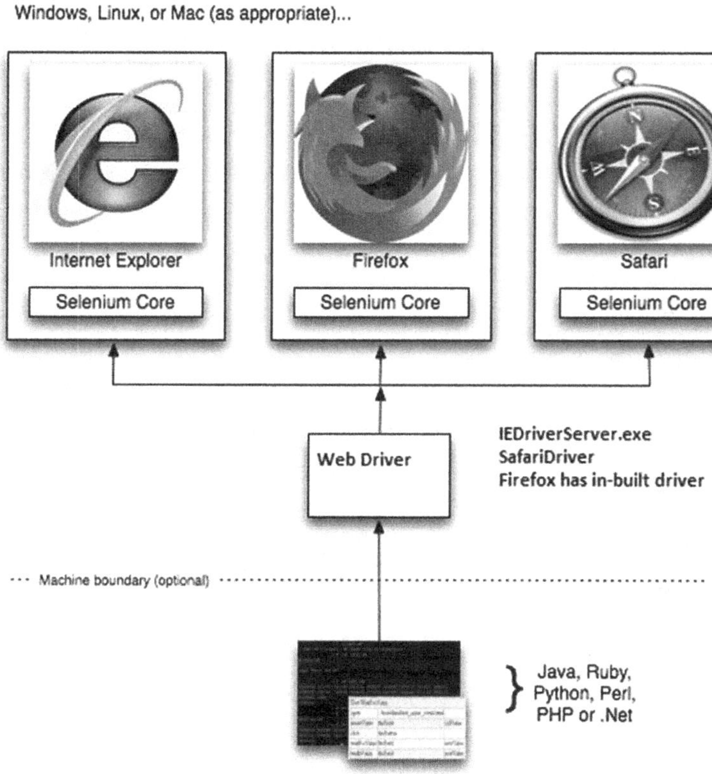

Windows, Linux, or Mac (as appropriate)...

Figure 2-1. *Selenium WebDriver architecture*

So, as you can see in Figure 2-1, as long as you write automation scripts that the intermediary server can understand (WebDriver), the server takes care of translating them into actual commands that emulate user actions on the browser.

How Does It Scale?

In Figure 2-1, you can see that a single intermediary server (chromedriver.exe, Driver Server.exe) can maintain the session with an active browser and execute commands that you direct in the automation scripts.

What if you want to execute tests in parallel? How about multiple instances of browsers on the same machine or on remote machines, and so on?

To solve the problem of parallel execution and leverage horizontal scaling, the Selenium Grid came into existence. Its architecture is shown in Figure 2-2.

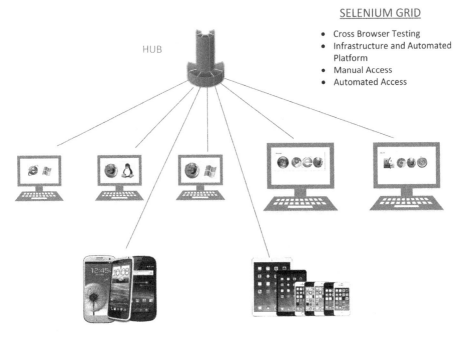

Figure 2-2. *The Selenium Grid*

A couple of noteworthy points:

- The HUB is an HTTP server that listens on a port and redirects the requests to the appropriate Grid node (which maps to a WebDriver).

- Since the communication happens on HTTP over TCP/IP, you can scale this model to the boundaries of the ports available on each machine in the control chain.

- The HUB is the entry point and communication between HUB and nodes is purely over REST APIs (GET, POST, etc.).

- The matching of a request from a client is done by the HUB based on the WebDriver protocol algorithm (a DesiredCapabilities object).

How Does It Relate to Mobile Automation?

Now, you can remotely execute commands on a browser as long as you have the intermediary server translating it to the right commands emulating user behavior.

The same concept is applied to mobile test automation. The Appium server is like a ChromeDriver, IEDriverServer, or Safari driver, in that it can communicate with the UI Automation library for the Android or iOS ecosystems.

Internally, Appium knows how to talk to the UIAutomation library for Android. The UIAutomation library will take commands from the Appium server and execute them on the app, which eventually translates to set, get, click, and all user actions.

As the author of automation scripts, as long as you know how to identify elements (various locator/selector strategies; this space is quite mature now) and perform operations on those elements, the intended behavior is automated.

Test Automation Libraries

Over the past few years, the test automation tools that got some traction for Android apps included MonkeyTalk, Robotium, UiAutomator (uses UI Automation library), calabash-android, selendroid, Appium, etc.

Android Espresso, a unit testing library that promises to do UI testing, is also relatively new as of writing this book. Let's wait and see how Expresso does; however, the fact that it is inside-out (unit testing) means that it might not cover the scope of integration testing (i.e., testing the exact path that an end user experiences).

This book uses Appium as the test automation tool/framework because I found it aligned with my needs of testing native, web, and hybrid apps. It also follows the WebDriver protocol. You can read Appium's philosophy and competitive analysis with other tools and frameworks on its web site (http://appium.io/introduction.html?lang=en).

Some tradeoffs between Appium and Espresso are as follows:

- Android Espresso is good because the tests are in the same language as the source code, which makes it easier to debug/troubleshoot and fosters collaboration among the technical staff (the dev and test engineers).

- If you need access to the source code, executing the tests may work fine, but requires multiple vetting of build pipelines. CI (and hence testing from outside) gives relatively higher confidence before release. Appium is a better choice in this regard.

- Use ATDD/BDD style because it lets lesser technical staff product owners/business stakeholders define "executable" acceptance criteria. This helps the three amigos (dev, test, and product) be on same page and fosters collaboration.

- Availability of developer's time, test coverage, etc., is also a tradeoff. Appium, with its support for most programming stacks, is a better choice in this regard.

Why Automate?

It should be a no-brainer why you automate processes. In fact, continuous integration and/or continuous delivery (see https://martinfowler.com/bliki/ContinuousDelivery.html) is *not* possible without automating the repeatable/mundane activities. Humans are not great compared to machines for computing repetitive tasks and performing all permutations and combinations on a certain problem.

That said, a human still has to architect and design the overall system, so should understand what a machine does and, more importantly, be able to troubleshoot when expected outcomes do not transpire.

For the mobile app space, this `article` shows the costs associated with resubmitting a mobile app. The numbers are only suggestive; in fact, the costs might be higher than what is displayed in the table. The point is to say that the costs associated with defects/bugs are very dear and include lost customers, countless developer hours, and brand image, to name a few.

Mobile Test Strategy

Software testers are familiar with writing test plans, test cases, and test release documents. A test strategy document is generally written by taking into account the application's operating environment, the release cycle, test coverage, defect tracking, and overall a document that can be presented to executive management for approval of budget and timelines. Mobile test strategy aims to carve out the how, why, and what aspects that affect mobile testing. The following sections include are few considerations for creating a mobile test strategy.

Manual Testing vs. Automation

There are very rare scenarios in which the human eye does significantly better than an automated program when validating software, such as the aesthetics of a web site. That gap is also getting narrower by the day. AI (artificial intelligence) and ML (machine learning), for example, provide a much better ROI in the age of speed and continuous delivery. Visual test automation by tools like Applitools is a great example. This is *not* to say that we should make manual testing function redundant in an organization, rather it is to say that testing capabilities should include both automation and manual approaches, with a focus on automation.

In the context of mobile testing, it is almost impossible for a human to manually test permutations and combinations across the dimensions of devices, SDKs, API levels, and ecosystems. Hence, your testing strategy should include (but not be limited to):

- Automate early and often in the bottom-up order of the testing pyramid (see the "Test Pyramid" section later in this chapter).

- Use BDD/TDD frameworks in the early stages when acceptance criteria are not clear and an automation script cannot be run (use mock frameworks to mitigate the absence of a real system).

- Building and deploying an app should be self-serviced and automated without any exceptions.

- Collaborate with other roles on the team and, in rare circumstances (such as during sprint demos), manually walk through workflows of the system (otherwise, the automation script should be run as a demo).

- The programming language should start with known, and tend toward the most collaborative.

- Inside-out/outside-in (focus on end users).

- Don't boil the ocean—pick one and pivot.

- Interoperability—cloud and on-premises infrastructures.

- Tend toward using real devices.

- Use Appium, Espresso, and XCTest.

Speed of Testing

High-speed testing is a mandatory requirement in the mobile space because a mobile app is successful in the market based on how fast it is delivered in the face of competition. There have been research studies suggesting that mobile users have an attention span of minutes before they uninstall an app. Releasing bug-free apps often is a make-or-break situation.

Scaling

Think of AWS and Netflix. The services can respond by scaling the systems based on load, performance, user traffic, and so on. While testing mobile apps, the testing capability should also be scalable across the three Vs (volume, variety, and velocity) with a tradeoff against cost. In the beginning of developing a project, it is advisable to rely on open source and cloud services before investing heavily on paid solutions.

Cost

Cost is a constraint in every decision you make when resources are required. Resources can be human, machine, time, etc. Hence, investing in open source solutions at the beginning is less risky because there is no vendor lock-in. It is a tradeoff decision because if you spend too much time on not-so-mature open source solutions, you might lose time. When it's all said and done, open source solutions have come a long way and are mature in many ways. In fact, they are much more mature than some paid solutions in some cases. Your strategy should be to spend a week or two and scour the web for solutions and frameworks that are already built and use one as a starting point.

Testing Pyramid

The testing pyramid helps in terms of having conversations around how much and what priorities do different kinds of testing have in a project. See Figure 2-3.

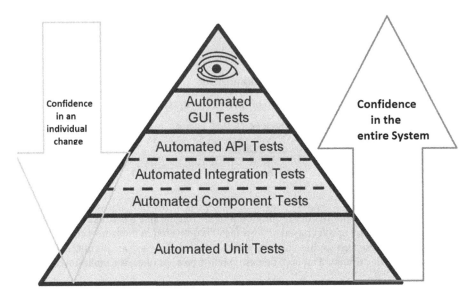

Figure 2-3. *The testing pyramid*

In the context of mobile testing (most mobile apps at the time of writing this book focus on the GUI layer), the pyramid can be read as follows:

- The confidence while building the app (work-in-progress) is enhanced with more tests at the bottom of the pyramid. Hence, automated unit tests that execute successfully give confidence that the unit/component is a higher quality.

- Since a software application is a network of components, integration points between the components become important as you race toward release to production.

- Finally, the user experiences the GUI of the mobile app, hence from a user's perspective, automated GUI tests give the highest confidence in quality. (For example, if a component at the lower layer breaks, the user's experience will be felt at the GUI layer.)

- The confidence in the overall system is enhanced by successfully running tests from lower to higher layers in the testing pyramid.

- The testing pyramid also articulates the relative volume of tests to be written at various layers of the application.

Further reading on the testing pyramid can be found at `http://www.seleniumframework.com/decision-models/choose-automation-solution-2/`.

Mobile Test Environment

Mobile apps like web apps need an environment to run on. The environment is a function of hardware and software. To test a mobile app's functionality, you need a mobile lab that can emulate a real-world scenario—i.e., a user operating on a mobile app and the workflows being executed. Mobile test environments can be complex to emulate, because the experience is controlled in a chain, and the individual links are owned by multiple entities. For example, the network bandwidth is controlled by the telecom providers, the software experience is controlled by Google and its Android partners, and so on. You'll explore the considerations that matter while interacting with a mobile test environment in the following sections.

Real Devices vs. Emulators/Simulators

One of the biggest challenges with mobile testing is device support. The number of models and the types of smartphones are increasing by the day and growing at an accelerating pace. There are differences between devices and which devices to test is not an easy challenge to solve. It is dependent on identifying the compatibility matrix as early as possible in the project, yet that becomes a challenge to collect as it is not static.

However, you need to start narrowing it all down with an initial list.

Emulators/simulators cannot emulate every feature of a real device—pixel perfect, phone hardware quirks, etc. In general, the software representation of underlying hardware in Android world is called an *emulator* (as opposed to a *simulator* in the iOS world).

The test environment for mobile devices involves a mix of real devices and emulators/simulators to get the test coverage you expect—of course, the tradeoff is with cost.

Initial Manual Testing on a Local Android Real Device

In the case of a local Android device, use the following steps to experience the first build of an app.

Android SDK installed on a Windows or Mac:

1. Insure that the SDK is updated with the latest device drivers. For the Mac, my experience has been relatively easier with the device drivers; however, with Windows, I had to explicitly install the driver by going to the handset device manufacturer's web site.

2. From the source code perspective, the attribute android:debuggable=true should be set.

3. On the actual device, navigate to Settings ➤ Developer Options ➤ Enable USB Debugging and set that to True. If the setting is not found, navigate to Settings ➤ About Phone and click Build Number seven times. That should bring up the option.

4. Once the device is connected, a dialog box will appear on the device. Accept the message to allow communication.

5. A quick verification step is to type adb devices from the terminal (the adb binary is located inside the SDK folder inside platform-tools directory).

Initial Manual Testing on a Local Android Emulator

Use the Android Virtual Device Manager to create various Android virtual devices with different devices, SDK versions, and many more hardware characteristics.

Invoke the emulator as follows:

- Navigate to Android SDK folder/tools/ to locate the emulator binary.

- The emulator -avd avd_name command invokes the previously created AVD.

- I found it easier to first create an AVD configuration from IDE like Eclipse or IntelliJ, because the workflow is easier and the complex details are abstracted.

Further Manual Testing in the Cloud

You already know that it is almost impossible to have every device, hardware, and software and maintain a full-blown heterogeneous mobile test environment, as well as certify all devices and emulators for your mobile app. As you scale, you have to depend on cloud services.

- Start using Sauce Labs. Sauce Labs natively supports Appium and that helps you be familiar with the tool for the next phase of automation.

- Perfecto mobile is a fast growing service in terms of its coverage for mobile real devices and worth taking a look if you are an enterprise, as the cost vs. benefit analysis works well for large companies.

- Amazon Device Lab has many options since early 2017 and the service is maturing with support for Appium and similar automation tools without leaving the context of Amazon Web Services Console.

- Google Device Lab is a great option, if you are invested fully in Android mobile apps. The Google quality of experience is instantly realized, but bear in mind that the Google Cloud is slowly adding support for software automation frameworks like Appium and Calabash and would take a little bit more time as that is the not the core area they focused on. The purpose of Device Lab is to provide access to real devices in the cloud, not necessarily compete with Sauce Labs and Perfecto.

CHAPTER 3

CI Pattern with Jenkins and Android

This chapter introduces architectural patterns and covers a specific continuous integration pattern that you will learn to implement in subsequent chapters. The chapter goes through high-level architecture images of the pattern to help you picture it mentally. As you progress through the chapter, you'll see the steps needed to configure the feedback loop(s) that help you model and implement the pattern. It is important to complete the tools installation described in Chapter 1 before starting this chapter.

What Is Continuous Integration?

Continuous integration (CI) is a development practice that requires developers to integrate code into a shared repository several times a day. Each check-in is then verified by an automated build, allowing teams to detect problems early. There are similar concepts, such as *continuous deployment* and *continuous delivery*. However, to keep this conversation simple, what I mean by continuous integration in this book involves integration of changes into the source code, building and deploying the binaries, and delivering the binaries to a target environment where end users can interact with the app.

Feedback Loops

As discussed in Chapter 1, feedback loops can be implemented using the Jenkins tool. Images are provided to give you an idea about each build step inside the Jenkins UI interface.

■ **Note**   I used Jenkins 1.642.1 version. If you installed a different version of Jenkins, make sure you select the free style job. The interface should be the same.

© Pradeep Macharla 2017

P. Macharla, *Android Continuous Integration*, DOI 10.1007/978-1-4842-2796-1_3

Feedback Loop 1: Build

Figure 3-1 shows the build feedback loop in the overall architecture diagram. This is where you build the app.

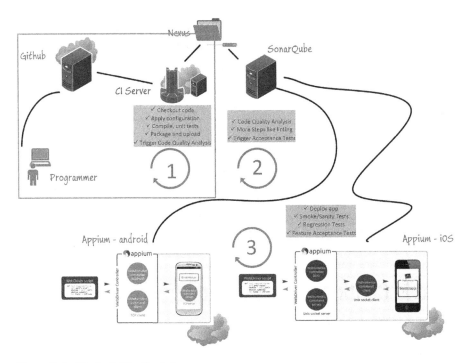

Figure 3-1. *The build feedback loop*

Based on the overall architecture, the first feedback loop does the following:

1. Checks out the code.

2. Applies (any) configuration.

3. Compiles.

4. Runs the unit tests (if any).

5. Packages and uploads the code.

6. Triggers the code quality analysis.

Jenkins Job1 Configuration

Figure 3-2 shows how a Jenkins Job is configured for the first feedback loop.
Name the Jenkins job and specify the Log Rotation strategy.

Figure 3-2. *The build job rotation*

Define an optional Boolean flag called UPLOAD to control the decision of uploading
the build artifact to Nexus. The default value is unchecked. If you check it, then the build
artifact gets uploaded to Nexus. See Figure 3-3.

Figure 3-3. *The build Nexus flag*

Enter the Nexus credentials to interact with Nexus; see Figure 3-4.

Figure 3-4. *The build Nexus credentials*

Enter the GitHub repository URL representing the source code, as shown in Figure 3-5.

Figure 3-5. *The build source control*

Check the boxes to delete the workspace before the build starts and to mask passwords, as shown in Figure 3-6.

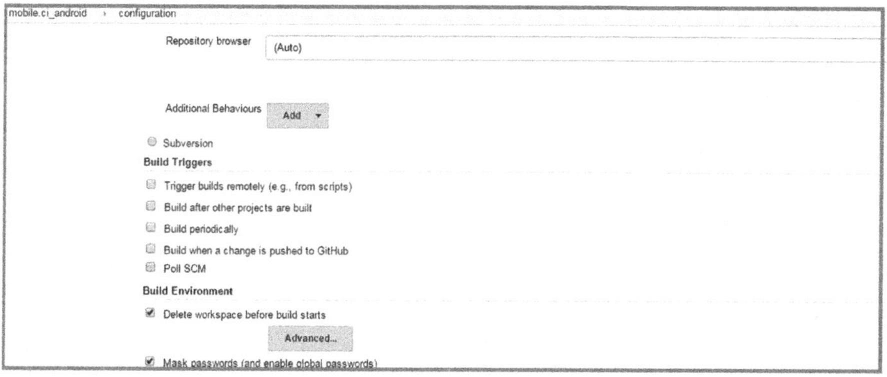

Figure 3-6. *The build workspace and mask password checkboxes*

Set the Nexus password as shown in Figure 3-7, so that it can be masked.

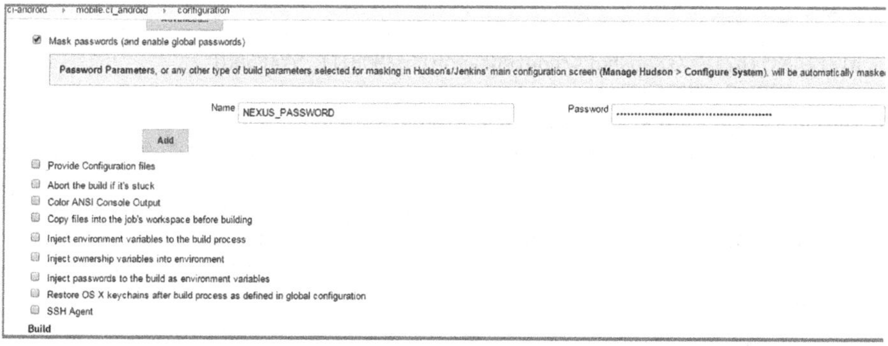

Figure 3-7. *The build Nexus password*

Set JAVA_HOME, ANDROID_HOME, GRADLE_HOME (see Figure 3-8 and the following code) and build the project. If any unit tests are written, execute that as the next build step. In this case, there are no unit tests. (Note: SONAR_RUNNER in this job is redundant; you'll use Sonar in a downstream Jenkins job.)

SSH Agent

Build

```
Execute shell

Command   #!/bin/bash
          ## uncomment set -xv for debuging
          #set -xv
          pwd
          ls -l
          export PATH=$PATH:$SONAR_RUNNER/bin

          export JDK_HOME=/Library/Java/JavaVirtualMachines/jdk1.8.0_65.jdk/contents/home/
          export JAVA_HOME=/Library/Java/JavaVirtualMachines/jdk1.8.0_65.jdk/contents/home
          export PATH=$PATH:$JDK_HOME/bin
          #Android
          export ANDROID_HOME=/Users/mobile-ci/documents/Android_SDK/android-sdk-r24.4.1
          export PATH=$PATH:$ANDROID_HOME/platform-tools
          export PATH=$PATH:$ANDROID_HOME/tools

          #Gradle
          GRADLE_HOME=/Users/mobile-ci/gradle-2.8
          export GRADLE_HOME
          export PATH=$PATH:$GRADLE_HOME/bin

          gradle clean assembleDebug
```

Figure 3-8. *The build Nexus password*

```
#!/bin/bash
## uncomment set -xv for debugging
#set -xv
export PATH=$PATH:$HOME/.rvm/bin
[[ -s "$HOME/.rvm/scripts/rvm" ]] && source "$HOME/.rvm/scripts/rvm"
pwd
rvm list
curl -u $NEXUS_USERNAME:$NEXUS_PASSWORD -O https://nexus.com/nexus/service/
local/repositories/snapshots/content-mobile/MOBILE_SNAPSHOT
tar xvzf MOBILE_SNAPSHOT
cp app-debug.apk ./features/support/resources
bundle exec cucumber features/android.feature DEVICE=$DEVICE -t @tag_name
```

Upload the build artifact (i.e., app-debug.apk) to Nexus so that it can be used further.

This example does not version this artifact with the Jenkins build number, because this is a snapshot. However, feel free to name the artifact aligned with your versioning strategy. See Figure 3-9.

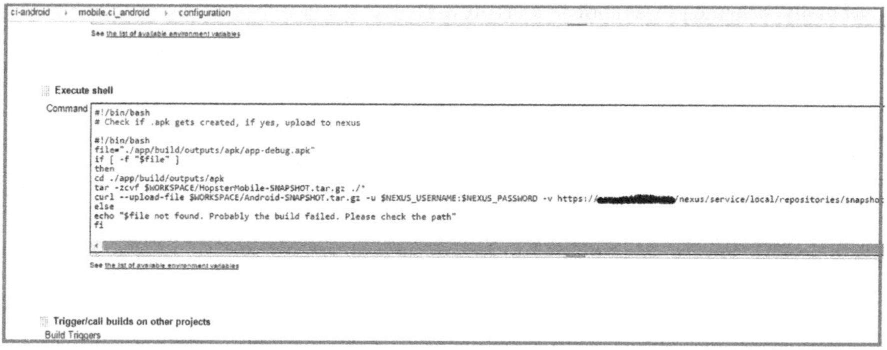

Figure 3-9. *The build upload artifact*

Kick off the downstream job to trigger SonarQube analysis, which is feedback loop 2. The UPSTREAM_BUILD_NUMBER strategy is to pass the value to the downstream job to pull the "correct" Nexus build artifact, as shown in Figure 3-10.

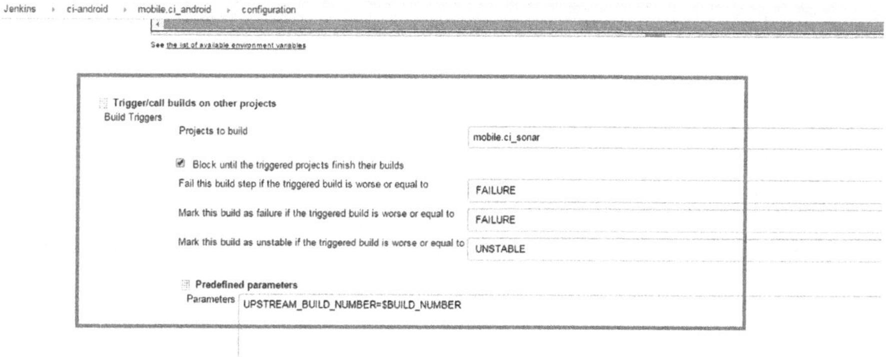

Figure 3-10. *The build trigger job*

Finally, save the job, as shown in Figure 3-11.

Figure 3-11. *The build save job*

Feedback (Execution Results)

After running the Jenkins job, the console output looks like this (see Figure 3-12 also):

```
:app:mergeDebugAssets
:app:generateDebugResValues
:app:generateDebugResources
:app:mergeDebugResources
:app:processDebugManifest
:app:processDebugResources
:app:generateDebugSources
:app:processDebugJavaRes UP-TO-DATE
:app:compileDebugJavaWithJavacNote: Some input files use or override a
deprecated API.
Note: Recompile with -Xlint:deprecation for details.
Note: /Users/mobile-ci/jenkins/workspace/mobile.android/app/src/main/java/
com/android/app/request/print/gc/GCGetPrinters.java uses unchecked or unsafe
operations.
Note: Recompile with -Xlint:unchecked for details.

:app:compileDebugNdk UP-TO-DATE
:app:compileDebugSources
:app:preDexDebug
:app:dexDebug
:app:validateDebugSigning
:app:packageDebug
:app:zipalignDebug
:app:assembleDebug

BUILD SUCCESSFUL

Total time: 1 mins 52.858 secs

This build could be faster, please consider using the Gradle Daemon:
https://docs.gradle.org/2.8/userguide/gradle_daemon.html
[mobile.android] $ /bin/bash /var/folders/m6/zpwf1w6sO4b_
ccjvm4175y4h0000gp/T/hudson7459346908680899717.sh
a ./app-debug-unaligned.apk
a ./app-debug.apk
  % Total  % Received % Xferd  Average Speed   Time    Time     Time  Current
                                 Dload  Upload   Total   Spent    Left  Speed

  0     0    0     0     0     0      0      0 --:--:-- --:--
:-- --:--:--     0*   Trying 192.168.1.71...
* Connected to nexus.server.com (192.168.1.71) port 443 (#0)
```

```
   0     0    0      0    0      0      0       0 --:--:-- --:--
:-- --:--:--      0* TLS 1.2 connection using TLS_DHE_RSA_WITH_AES_256_CBC_SHA
* Server certificate: *.company.com
* Server certificate: Go Daddy Secure Certificate Authority - G2
* Server certificate: Go Daddy Root Certificate Authority - G2
* Server auth using Basic with user 'jenkins'
> PUT /nexus/service/local/repositories/snapshots/content-mobile/MOBILE_
SNAPSHOT HTTP/1.1
> Host: nexus.server.com
> Authorization: Basic amVua2luczpJbm1hcjIwMTU=
> User-Agent: curl/7.43.0
> Accept: */*
> Content-Length: 24952303
> Expect: 100-continue
>
< HTTP/1.1 100 Continue
} [16384 bytes data]

 22 23.7M    0    0   22 5536k      0  5327k  0:00:04  0:00:01  0:00:03 5323k
 64 23.7M    0    0   64 15.2M      0  7670k  0:00:03  0:00:02  0:00:01 7670k*
We are completely uploaded and fine
< HTTP/1.1 201 Created
< Server: nginx/1.1.19
< Date: Tue, 08 Dec 2015 16:00:35 GMT
< Content-Length: 0
< Connection: keep-alive
< X-Frame-Options: SAMEORIGIN
< X-Content-Type-Options: nosniff
```

```
_android   ▸  #15
    :app:mergeDebugAssets
    :app:generateDebugResValues
    :app:generateDebugResources
    :app:mergeDebugResources
    :app:processDebugManifest
    :app:processDebugResources
    :app:generateDebugSources
    :app:processDebugJavaRes UP-TO-DATE
    :app:compileDebugJavaWithJavacNote: Some input files use or override a deprecated API.
    Note: Recompile with -Xlint:deprecation for details.
    Note: /Users/mobile-
    ci/jenkins/workspace/mobile.hopster_android/app/src/main/java/com/inmar/android/app/hopster/reque
    etPrinters.java uses unchecked or unsafe operations.
    Note: Recompile with -Xlint:unchecked for details.

    :app:compileDebugNdk UP-TO-DATE
    :app:compileDebugSources
    :app:preDexDebug
    :app:dexDebug
    :app:validateDebugSigning
    :app:packageDebug
    :app:zipalignDebug
    :app:assembleDebug

    BUILD SUCCESSFUL

    Total time: 1 mins 52.858 secs

    This build could be faster, please consider using the Gradle Daemon:
    https://docs.gradle.org/2.8/userguide/gradle_daemon.html
    [mobile.hopster_android] $ /bin/bash
    /var/folders/m6/zpwf1w6s04b_ccjvm4175y4h0000gp/T/hudson7459346908680899717.sh
```

Figure 3-12. Build results

Feedback Loop 2: Code Quality Analysis

The second feedback loop is the code quality analysis process using SonarQube, as shown in Figure 3-13.

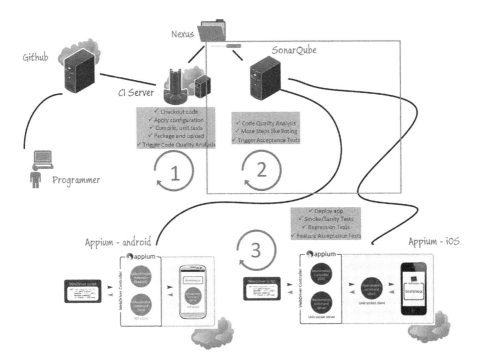

Figure 3-13. *Sonar feedback loop*

Jenkins Job 2: Sonar

Name the Jenkins job and define the Log Rotation strategy, as shown in Figure 3-14.

Figure 3-14. *Sonar job rotation*

Specify where the Sonar runner is available, as shown in Figure 3-15.

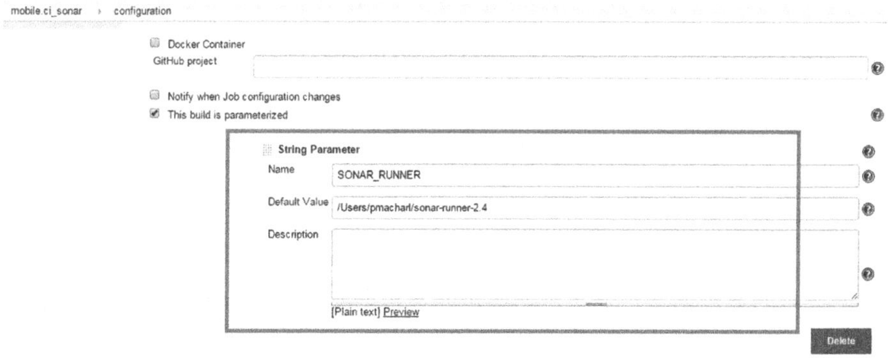

Figure 3-15. *Sonar runner*

Restrict where the project can be run and then download the source code. See Figure 3-16.

Figure 3-16. *Sonar source code*

Specify the checkout strategy, as shown in Figure 3-17.

Figure 3-17. *Sonar checkout*

Here you don't have `sonar-project.properties` inside the source code, so you can download it from Jenkins config file store and then add it to the check-out folder. See Figure 3-18.

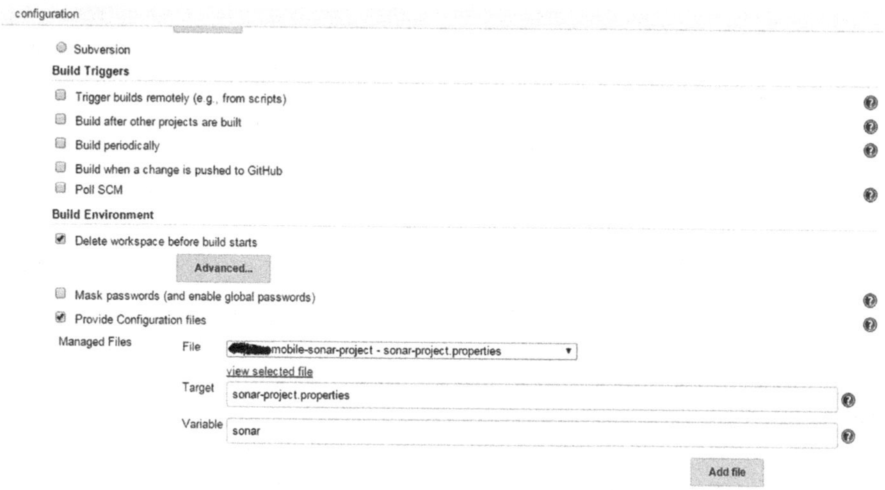

Figure 3-18. *Sonar project properties*

Since the config files are generally copied to the Jenkins master, you can move them to the build machine and hence use the $sonar variable as a carrier. See Figure 3-19.

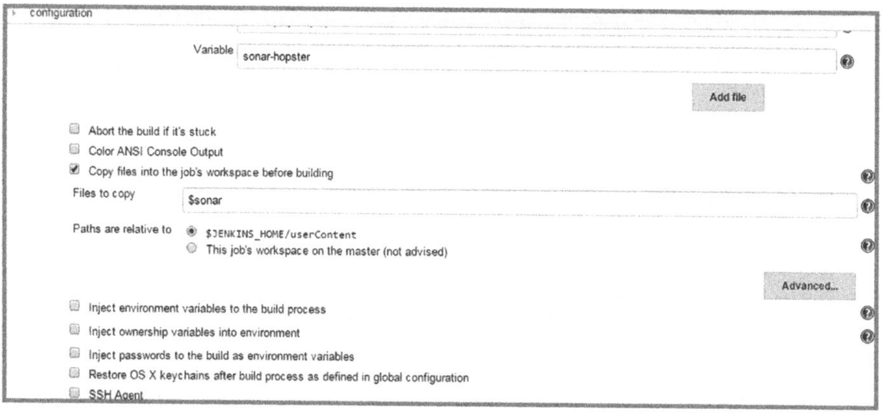

Figure 3-19. *Sonar job rotation*

You add a build step using the SonarQube plugin for Jenkins and configure it to use the sonar-runner, as defined on the Jenkins System configuration page. See Figure 3-20.

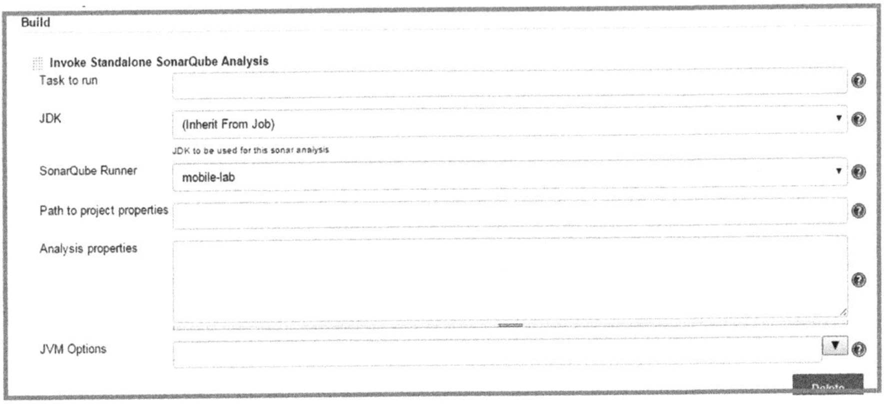

Figure 3-20. *Sonar job rotation feedback (execution results)*

After you run the job, the Jenkins console log looks like Figure 3-21.

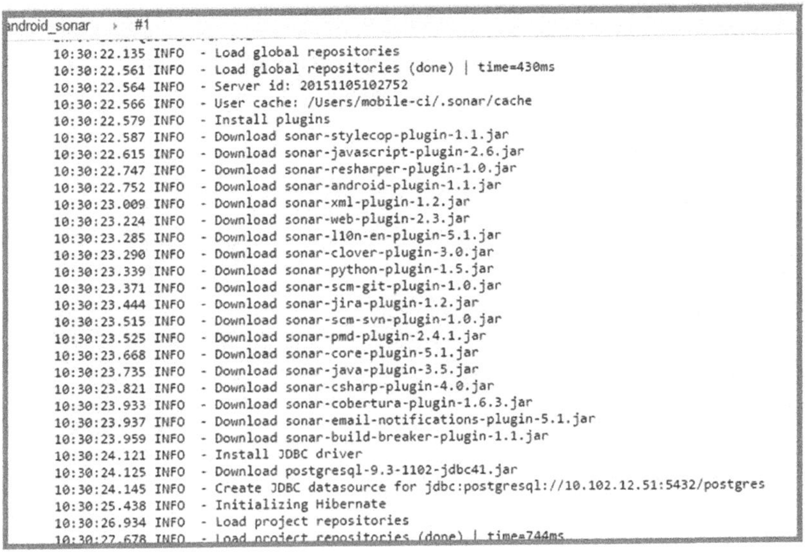

Figure 3-21. *Sonar console output*

Click the SonarQube icon. It will open the SonarQube home page/dashboard as you have configured it on the server. See Figure 3-22.

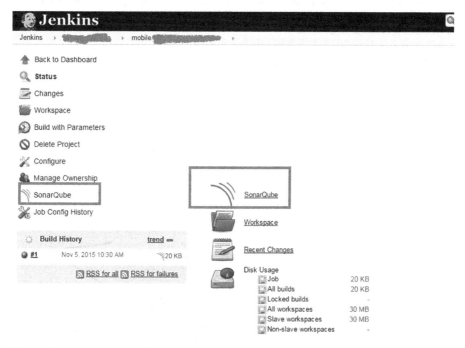

Figure 3-22. *Sonar icon link*

Figure 3-23 shows the Sonar Dashboard and each of the orange highlights (and many more hyperlinks) opens information that contains great feedback for developers.

Figure 3-23. *Sonar Dashboard*

Feedback Loop 3: Test

This feedback loop is the integration automation test—i.e., the acceptance tests that an end user would experience (see Figure 3-24). This is the relative difficult part to automate, so I discuss it in detail in Chapter 8.

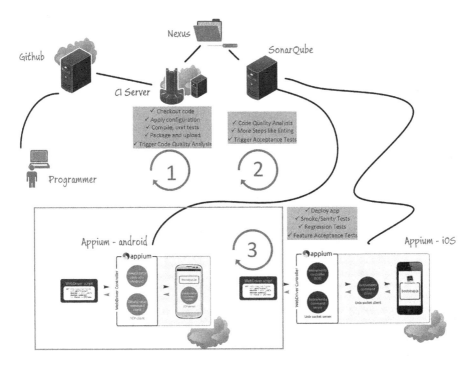

Figure 3-24. *Test feedback loop*

Jenkins Job 3: Acceptance Tests

Name the Jenkins job as smoke tests/acceptance tests, depending on how many you want to execute. This example uses smoke tests, as shown in Figure 3-25.

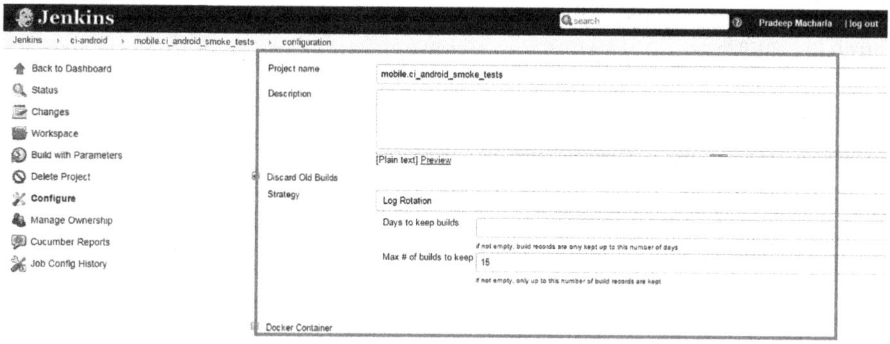

Figure 3-25. *Test job rotation*

Enter the Nexus username if you want to upload the results of the test execution (this example does not). Then define the DEVICE string parameter and add all the devices that are defined in the devices.yaml file in the acceptance tests projects. See Figure 3-26.

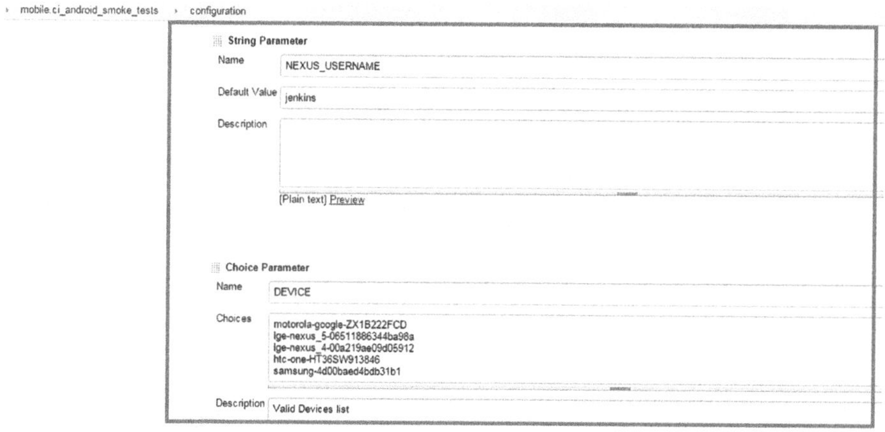

Figure 3-26. *Test Nexus and device parameters*

Specify where the project should run and download the acceptance tests code, as shown in Figure 3-27.

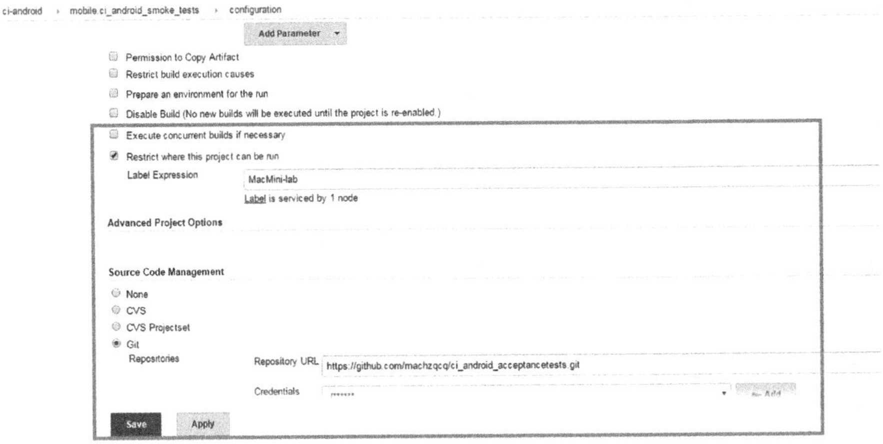

Figure 3-27. *Test source code*

Specify the master branch for code checkout, as shown in Figure 3-28.

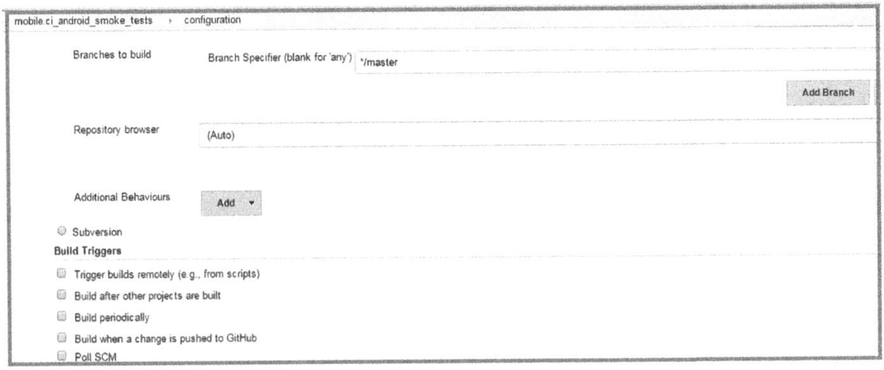

Figure 3-28. *Test Nexus and device parameters*

For Ruby dependencies, pull gems from the Nexus repo. You must then specify the Nexus access credentials, as shown in Figure 3-29.

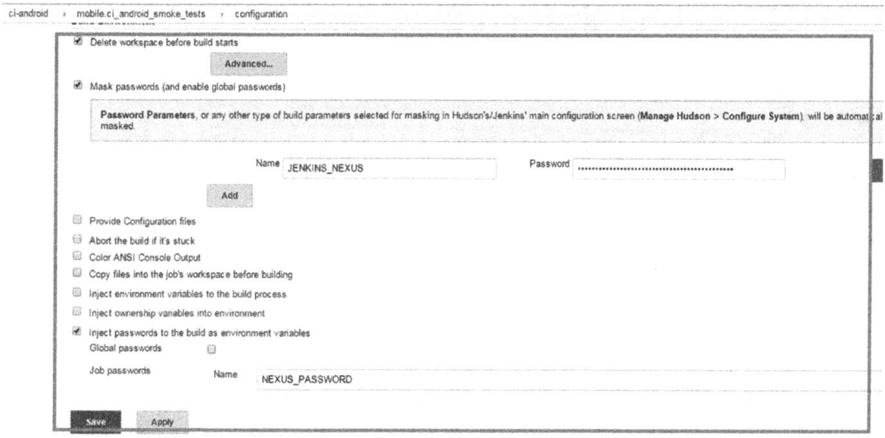

Figure 3-29. *Test Nexus access for Jenkins*

Download the app from Nexus, place it in the resources folder, and then execute the acceptance tests. See Figure 3-30.

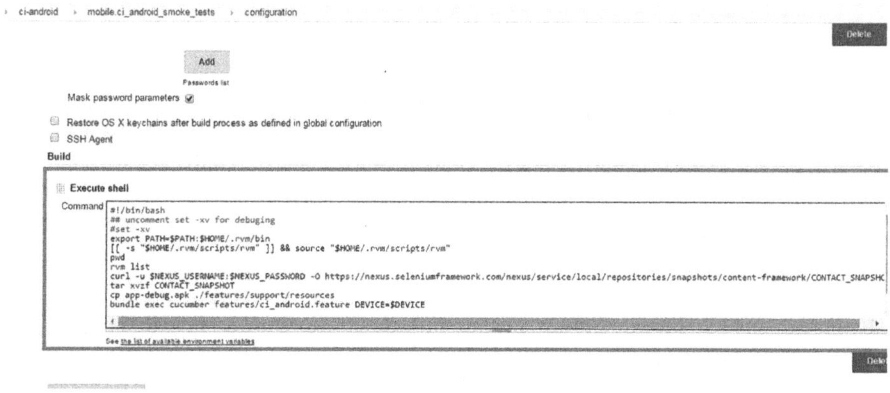

Figure 3-30. *Test Nexus and device parameters*

```
#!/bin/bash
## uncomment set -xv for debuging
#set -xv
export PATH=$PATH:$HOME/.rvm/bin
[[ -s "$HOME/.rvm/scripts/rvm" ]] && source "$HOME/.rvm/scripts/rvm"
pwd
echo $UPSTREAM_BUILD_NUMBER
rvm list
curl -u$NEXUS_USERNAME:$NEXUS_PASSWORD -O https://nexus.inmar.com/nexus/
service/local/repositories/snapshots/content-mobile/HOPSTER_MOBILE_
SNAPSHOT_$UPSTREAM_BUILD_NUMBER
ls -l
bundle exec cucumber features/android.feature:19 DEVICE=$DEVICE
```

Choose Publish Cucumber Results as a Report, as shown in Figure 3-31.

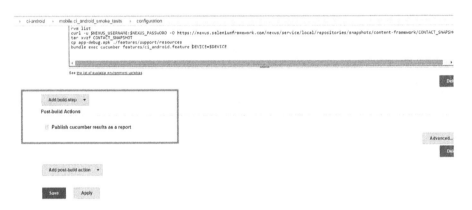

Figure 3-31. *Test publish Cucumber results*

Feedback (Execution Results)

Since you choose to publish the Cucumber results as a report, you can get reports, as shown in Figures 3-32 and 3-33.

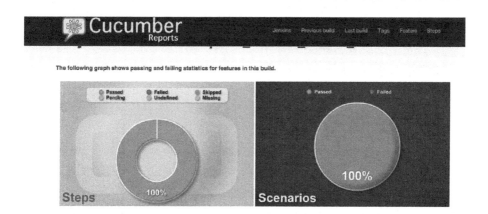

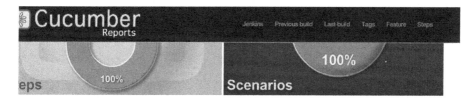

ature Statistics

Feature	Scenarios			Steps							Duration	Status
	Total	Passed	Failed	Total	Passed	Failed	Skipped	Pending	Undefined	Missing		
ter Android	2	2	0	4	4	0	0	0	0	0	20s 821ms	passed
1	2	2	0	4	4	0	0	0	0	0	20s 821ms	Totals

Figure 3-32. *Test Cucumber graphical reports-1*

45

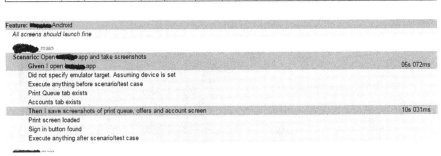

Figure 3-33. *Test cumber graphical reports-2*

CHAPTER 4

Android System Setup

Chapter 3 focused on how fast you can get to a quick feedback loop, and this chapter covers what is needed for an MVP. The Android world has great tools and utilities that address the varied needs of a developer.

You will install the following so that you can learn to build an app:

- Java
- Android SDK
- Android Studio
- Gradle

Installing Java

This section explains the Java platform and how to install it.

JRE vs. JDK vs. SE

You will download and install the Java Development Kit (JDK) in this section. As a quick refresher, you might wonder which Java package you need.

- **JDK:** Software developers generally tend to use the JDK. It includes the Java runtime and libraries for troubleshooting and monitoring applications.

- **SE (Standard Edition):** Administrators typically use the SE version.

- **JRE (Java Runtime Environment):** This is the minimal version used by end users to run Java applications.

© Pradeep Macharla 2017

P. Macharla, *Android Continuous Integration*, DOI 10.1007/978-1-4842-2796-1_4

JDK on Mac

To install the JDK on your Mac, you simply accept the license agreement, download the
.dmg file, and install it, as shown in Figure 4-1.

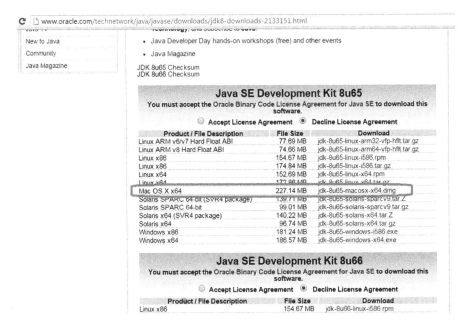

Figure 4-1. *JDK download for the Mac*

After installing and making modifications to ~/.profile, you'll see something
similar to the output shown in Figure 4-2. Ensure that the Java executable is available
on the path and that the shell variables $JAVA_HOME, $JDK_HOME, and $PATH are updated
as shown.

Figure 4-2. *Shell variables*

```
export JDK_HOME=/Library/Java/JavaVirtualMachines/jdk1.8.0_60.jdk/Contents/Home
export JAVA_HOME=$(usr/libexec/java_home)
export PATH=$PATH:$JDK_HOME/bin
```

Installing Android SDK

Android SDK tools can be installed from the Android developer site. If you are a developer, it makes more sense to download Android Studio (which comes bundled with the SDK). However, if you are a devops/build/release/CI engineer, you might want to do things *headless*, so it makes more sense to download the standalone tools.

This book focuses more on doing things headless, because IDEs in the background mostly call the commands.

Standalone SDK

Download the standalone SDK from `https://developer.android.com/studio/index.html`. Navigate to the bottom of the page for installing the tools, as shown in Figure 4-3.

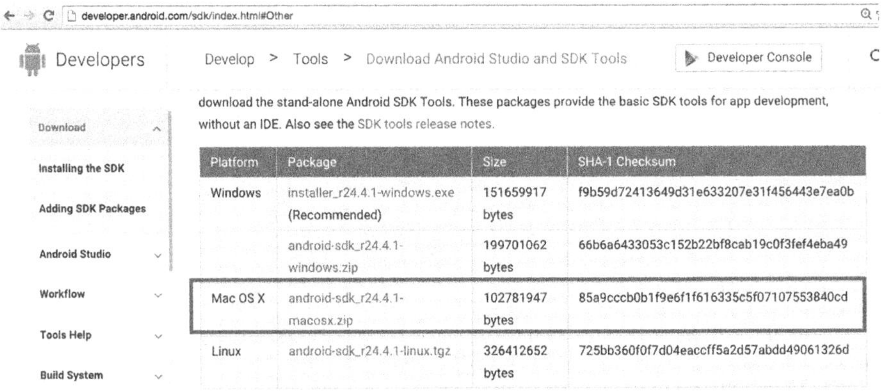

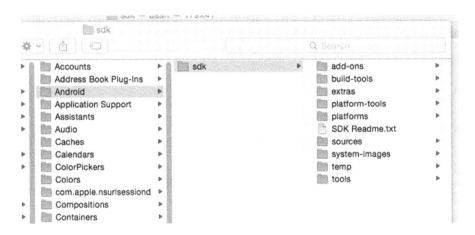

Figure 4-3. *Android SDK download*

The contents are extracted to the `/Users/pmacharl/Library/Android/sdk` folder, as shown in Figure 4-4.

Figure 4-4. *Android SDK folder view*

Now add these shell variables to the ~/.profile path (see Figure 4-5):

- ANDROID_HOME=/Users/pmacharl/Library/Android/sdk

- PATH=$PATH:$ANDROID_HOME/platform-tools

- PATH=$PATH:$ANDROID_HOME/tools

```
Anyones-Mac-mini:sdk pmacharl$ cat ~/.profile
export JDK_HOME=/Library/Java/JavaVirtualMachines/jdk1.8.0_60.jdk/Contents/Home
export JAVA_HOME=$(usr/libexec/java_home)
export PATH=$PATH:$JDK_HOME/bin
#Android
export ANDROID_HOME=/Users/pmacharl/Library/Android/sdk
export PATH=$PATH:$ANDROID_HOME/platform-tools
export PATH=$PATH:$ANDROID_HOME/tools

#Gradle
GRADLE_HOME=/Users/pmacharl/Installations/gradle-2.7
export GRADLE_HOME
export PATH=$PATH:$GRADLE_HOME/bin

#Appium

export PATH="$PATH:$HOME/.rvm/bin" # Add RVM to PATH for scripting

[[ -s "$HOME/.rvm/scripts/rvm" ]] && source "$HOME/.rvm/scripts/rvm" # Load RVM into a shell session *as a function*
Anyones-Mac-mini:sdk pmacharl$ []
```

Figure 4-5. *Update shell variables*

Quick Checks

Since you will use the adb and uiautomatorviewer executables in subsequent sections, it's smart to check that they are available in the PATH now.

Type uiatomatorviewer, as shown in Figure 4-6.

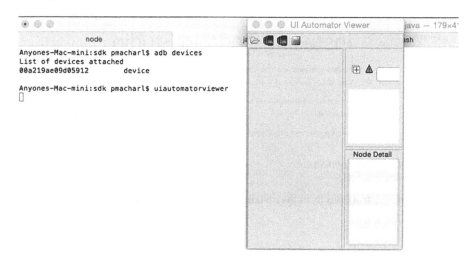

Figure 4-6. *uiautomatorviewer*

Press Ctrl+C in the shell or close uiautomatorviewer directly.

This ensures that you have Android SDK set up and ready for building apps.

Installing Android Studio

In the previous section, you installed the Android SDK as a standalone and made it available to your build environments by setting the PATH variables.

In this section, you will learn how to install and set up Android Studio.

■ **Note** Android Studio is *not* required for building, deploying, or testing apps. It is a developer environment that enables you to develop apps.

There are many benefits to having Android Studio, because the IDE centralizes accessibility of features like updating the SDK, adb, the device monitor, looking at logs, and more. Hence, it is strongly recommended that you install Android Studio even though it's not required.

Download it from https://developer.android.com/studio/index.html. See Figure 4-7.

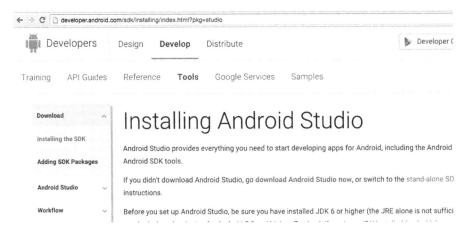

Figure 4-7. Install Android Studio

Follow the instructions from the installer and go with the defaults.

Android Studio Basics

In this section, you will walk through some of the functionalities in Android Studio that matter to the use cases in this book. Just follow along and click through at this stage in the book.

Open an Android project. Point to the Android project that you are working on, as shown in Figure 4-8.

Figure 4-8. *Open the Android project*

Hover over the icons shown in Figure 4-9 and click each to get a feel for navigating in Android Studio.

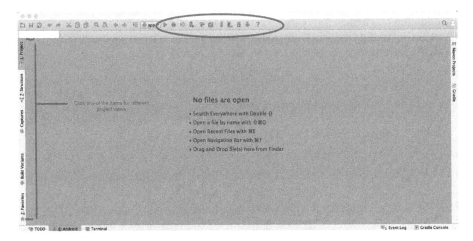

Figure 4-9. *Android Studio subtools*

Hovering over the icons highlighted in Figure 4-9 shows you options related to the following:

- **AVD Manager:** This will launch AVD manager. You will learn how to create emulators and manage Android virtual devices in another section.

- **SDK Manager:** This will help you manage all updates to the Android SDK.

- **Android Device Monitor:** This will let you monitor your Android device when connected and talking to adb.

Associate the System SDK with Android Studio

By default, Android Studio comes bundled with Android SDK. However, if you are already using an SDK bundle (as mentioned in previous section, if you already have SDK downloaded and set in another folder), then point it to that.

■ **Note** Remember that this book uses an SDK downloaded separately because you need the flexibility to be able to build, deploy, and test the examples with and without Android Studio.

At the top left, choose Android Studio ➤ Preferences to open up this page. Edit the value to point to the folder where you downloaded the Android SDK. See Figure 4-10.

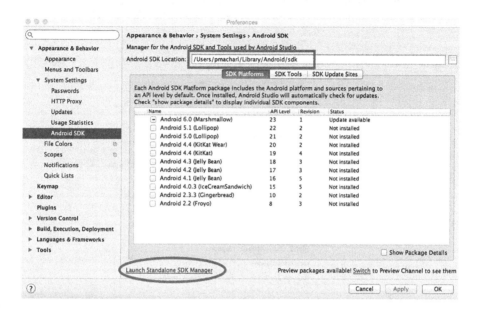

Figure 4-10. *Associate SDK with Android Studio*

Installing Gradle

Gradle is a build package manager that helps dependency management when building Android apps. Compare it with Ant, Maven, npm, Rake, etc.

Download and Install

Download the binary from `https://gradle.org/gradle-download/`. It is an archive, so you need to extract the contents to a folder on your machine. See Figure 4-11.

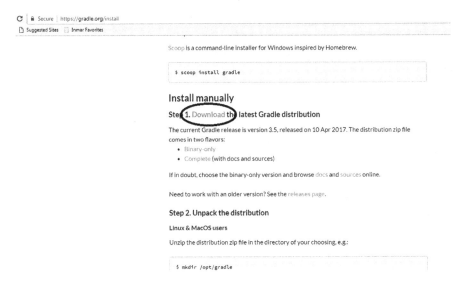

Figure 4-11. *Download Gradle*

Figure 4-12 shows where it looks after it's extracted. The version being used is 2.7, but you should download the latest version you can. There are not too many differences that will affect your Android app build.

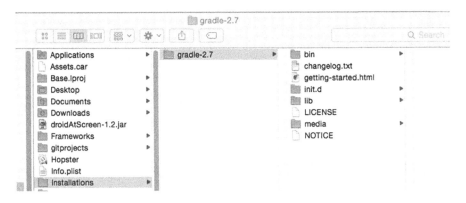

Figure 4-12. *Gradle folder structure*

Set Gradle Shell Variables

Add the following code to your ~/.profile so that the Gradle binary is available in $PATH and $GRADLE_HOME is available when building the Android app. See Figure 4-13.

```
node                              bash                              bash                    pmacharl@CORP
Anyones-Mac-mini:sdk pmacharl$ cat ~/.profile
export JDK_HOME=/Library/Java/JavaVirtualMachines/jdk1.8.0_60.jdk/Contents/Home
export JAVA_HOME=$(usr/libexec/java_home)
export PATH=$PATH:$JDK_HOME/bin
#Android
export ANDROID_HOME=/Users/pmacharl/Library/Android/sdk
export PATH=$PATH:$ANDROID_HOME/platform-tools
export PATH=$PATH:$ANDROID_HOME/tools

#Gradle
GRADLE_HOME=/Users/pmacharl/Installations/gradle-2.7
export GRADLE_HOME
export PATH=$PATH:$GRADLE_HOME/bin

#Appium

export PATH="$PATH:$HOME/.rvm/bin" # Add RVM to PATH for scripting

[[ -s "$HOME/.rvm/scripts/rvm" ]] && source "$HOME/.rvm/scripts/rvm" # Load RVM into a shell session *as a function*
```

Figure 4-13. *Gradle shell variables*

```
GRADLE_HOME=/Users/pmacharl/Installations/gradle-2.7
export GRADLE_HOME
export PATH=$PATH:$GRADLE_HOME/bin
```

Android Studio with Gradle

Android Studio comes bundled with Gradle and uses its own version internally. If you are a developer, you might find it more comfortable to use the built-in version so that you don't have to manage yet another tool.

Since you need the flexibility to do this with an IDE and do it in the CI (headless) way for this book's examples, I suggest you direct Android Studio to use the Gradle downloaded previously, as shown in Figure 4-14.

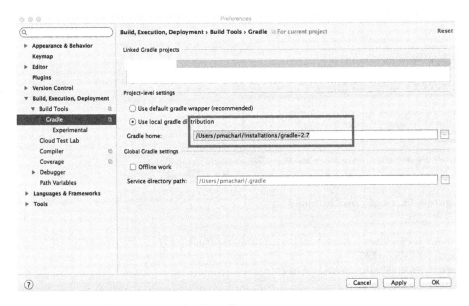

Figure 4-14. *Gradle setting in Android Studio*

Gradle Quick Commands

gradle --help will give you the options for quick commands.

Gradle Tasks

Gradle works by executing tasks. There can be two types:

- **Built-in tasks**: Come by default
- **Gradle custom tasks:** Craft your own tasks

You will use the built-in tasks to start with. It's beyond the scope of this chapter to go into the details of writing custom tasks.

Built-in tasks are categorized into the following areas:

- Android tasks

- Build tasks

- Build Setup tasks

- Help tasks

- Install tasks

- Verification tasks

- Other tasks

To see all the tasks and more detail, run `gradle tasks --all`.
To see more details about a task, run `gradle help --task`.

Build the App

Gradle generally looks for a `build.gradle` file in the current directory and parses the file to follow the instructions.

In this book, you will build the app using the following command, which runs inside the Android project root directory:

```
gradle clean assembleDebug
```

I will go into details about building the app from the project in subsequent chapters.

■ **Note** If you do not want to worry about managing Gradle versions (downloading, extracting, and ensuring the right version is used), you can use the Gradle wrapper. The Gradle wrapper comes bundled with Gradle. The only change is, instead of using the `gradle` binary, you use the `gradlew` binary in the same folder.

Tools to Know

Some of the Android SDK tools that I found useful (from the perspective of CI) are:

- ADB (Android Debug Bridge)

- Record Video

- uiautomatorviewer

- AVD Manager

- SDK Manager

- Device Monitor

The next few sections cover how to use these tools.

ADB

Android Debug Bridge (adb) is a client that runs on a developer box and instructs a component that runs on the developer box, which in turn communicates with a daemon that runs either on an emulator or on a real device.

Here is an example of an adb command. It lists the number of devices connected to the machine on which adb is executed.

```
pradeep@seleniumframework.com:~ pmacharl$ adb devices
List of devices attached
00a219ae09d05912    device
```

This is one of the most important tools that I recommend you learn to use. You will use adb to communicate with the app on the emulator/real device, to install the app, and to accomplish many other feats.

Here are some adb commands that I use extensively:

- adb devices lists all emulators and devices that can communicate with this adb server.

- adb install <apk> installs apk on the one emulator/device that is available to the adb server.

- adb install -e <serial_number> <apk> installs apk on a targeted emulator or device.

- adb kill-server kills the adb server. I use this when the server is in an unstable state.

- adb start-server starts the adb server.

It will be very beneficial to go over the complete list of options that adb provides, especially when you're troubleshooting. I recommend the official page, found at https://www.gitbook.com/book/machzqcq/ci-automation-mobileapps/edit.

You will use the previous commands when you build-deploy-test the CI pattern in a later chapter.

Record Video

From Android Kitkat, i.e. 4.4 version and above, adb provides a way to record screen video and save it to the device storage. You can pull the video to the local system from there.

Here are the steps for screen recording and saving:

1. Start adb shell screenrecord /path.

2. Recording starts and waits until you no longer need to record the screen.

3. Press Ctrl+C in the shell to stop recording.

4. Pull the video to your local filesystem.

```
pradeep@seleniumframework.com $ adb shell screenrecord /sdcard/example.mp4 ^C
pradeep@seleniumframework.com $ adb pull /sdcard/example.mp4
4972 KB/s (2900775 bytes in 0.569s)
```

uiautomatorviewer

From the perspective of an automation engineer, uiautomatorviewer is very similar to Chrome's dev-tools, Firefox's dev-tools, etc. Writing web-based automation code (such as with Selenium), identifying HTML elements (like ID, name, and other properties), and passing that as input to identify objects is very similar to what you can achieve with uiautomatorviewer, but on the mobile side. Figure 4-15 shows the interface.

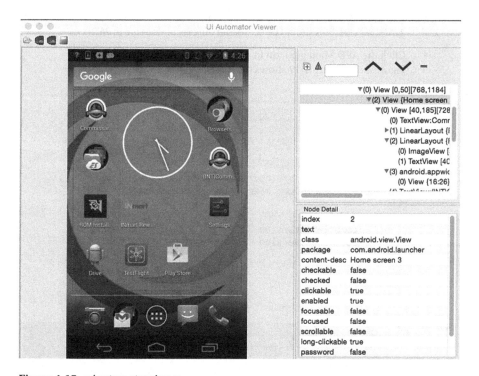

Figure 4-15. *uiautomatorviewer*

Some notes about uiautomatorviewer:

- It's generally located in the $ANDROID_HOME/tools directory.

- You launch it by typing uiautomatorviewer.

- Figure 4-15 is taken by clicking the Device Screenshot button, which is the second icon from the left.

- You can see the XML hierarchy of the elements and each node property in the node detail. This is useful when you're writing Appium automated tests (if you want to use uiautomatorviewer).

- You can save a screenshot using this tool.

AVD Manager

The AVD Manager provides a graphical user interface in which you can create and manage Android Virtual Devices (AVDs), which are required by the Android Emulator.

Launch AVD Manager using either of these options (one is from the command line and the other is from Android Studio):

- Run the android avd command at the command line. It launches avd (shell variables should be set so that the executables are in PATH).

- Click the AVD Manager icon in Android Studio IDE, as shown in Figure 4-16. Figure 4-17 shows the AVDs.

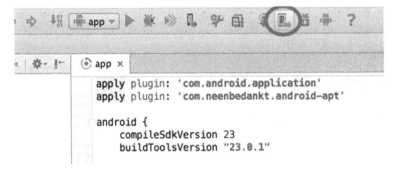

```
apply plugin: 'com.android.application'
apply plugin: 'com.neenbedankt.android-apt'

android {
    compileSdkVersion 23
    buildToolsVersion "23.0.1"
```

Figure 4-16. *AVD Manager*

Type	Name	Resolution	API	Target	CPU/ABI	Size on Disk	Actions
	Nexus 4 API 23	768 × 1280: xhdpi	23	Google APIs	x86	1 GB	▶ ✎ ▾
	Nexus 4 API 23 x86	768 × 1280: xhdpi	23	Google APIs	x86	1 GB	▶ ✎ ▾

+ Create Virtual Device...

Figure 4-17. *AVD Manager with AVDs*

When you start to understand the Android world, you want a sandbox to play with. Android Virtual Device Manager lets you create AVDs/emulators for different hardware and software configurations. I found the following features beneficial while learning the platform:

- You can create emulators for phones, tablets, wearing, TV, etc.

- You can play with different form factors, screen resolutions, and sizes.

- You can experiment with different memory sizes, API levels of software, cameras, sensors, etc.

Sure, there is no substitute for a real device, but emulators at least help you understand the various configuration(s) available, as well as identify which ones matter while developing, building, and testing the apps. More domain knowledge for the engineers means a higher chance of a better quality app.

SDK Manager

The Android SDK Manager (see Figure 4-18) separates the SDK tools, platforms, and other components into packages for easy access and management.

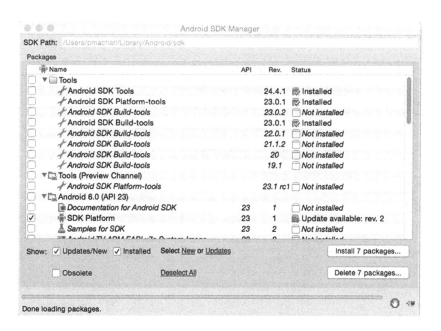

Figure 4-18. *SDK Manager*

Launch SDK Manager using one of these options (one is from the command line and the other is from Android Studio):

- Run the `android sdk` command from the command line. It launches the SDK manager (the shell variables should be set so that the executables are in PATH). See `https://www.gitbook.com/book/machzqcq/ci-automation-mobileapps/edit` for more information.

- Click the SDK Manager icon in the Android Studio IDE, as shown in Figure 4-19. Figure 4-20 shows the result.

Figure 4-19. *SDK Manager: Android Studio icon*

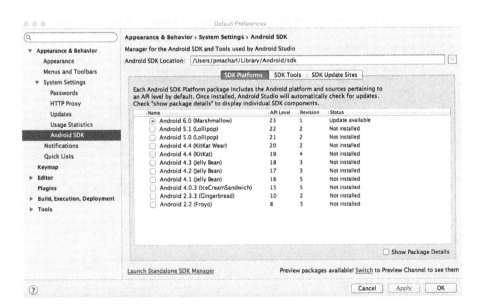

Figure 4-20. *SDK Manager: Android Studio*

Android Device Monitor

Android Device Monitor is a standalone tool that provides a graphical user interface for several Android application debugging and analysis tools.

Launch SDK Manager using one of these options (one is from the command line and the other is from Android Studio):

- Run the `monitor` command from the command line. It launches the device monitor (shell variables should be set so that the executables are in `PATH`). See `https://www.gitbook.com/book/machzqcq/ci-automation-mobileapps/edit` for more information).

- Click the Device Monitor icon in the Android Studio IDE, as shown in Figure 4-21.

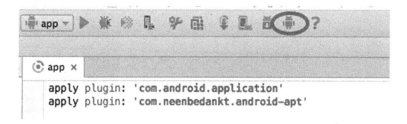

Figure 4-21. *Device Monitor: Android Studio*

You can see the view when one device is connected in Figure 4-22.

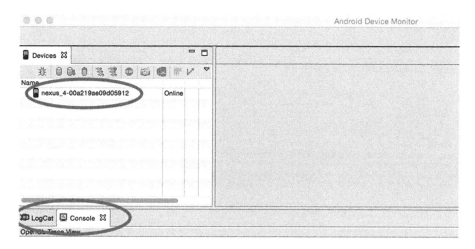

Figure 4-22. *Device Monitor: device connected*

CHAPTER 5

■ ■ ■

Build the Android App

The Android app can be built in debug or release mode—the difference being the keystore used to sign the app. If you build the app in release mode, the keystore will let you push to Google Play (assuming that the keystore associated with the user ID has already been registered through Google Play).

Since the CI process requires building many times before being ready to be release, this chapter shows you how to build the app in debug mode and use the .apk that's generated to pass it to the CI test automation step.

The Android Build Process

The following section contains a quick, high-level architecture overview of the Android app build process. Minor variations might exist in your specific projects.

Overview

Understanding the build process and being able to tweak it to suit your requirements is necessary once you have an MVP. I am a big fan of building the thin slice first, although there are many inefficiencies that can exist in the process. Once you see the result, the confidence and optimism will motivate you to go back and optimize the process. This is a good way to keep the stakeholders happy too, because it demonstrates continuous progress. Figure 5-1 shows an overview of the build process.

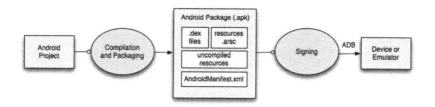

Figure 5-1. *The Android build process*

© Pradeep Macharla 2017

P. Macharla, *Android Continuous Integration*, DOI 10.1007/978-1-4842-2796-1_5

Another Perspective on the Build Process

Consider another perspective with Gradle, which is a build and packaging tool that drives the build process.

Figure 5-2 shows this build process.

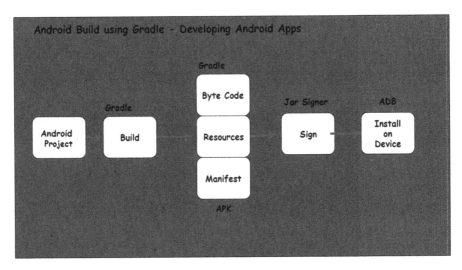

Figure 5-2. *Android build process with Gradle*

Output of the Build Process

After successfully building the app from the source code, you'll generally be interested in the .apk file, which is the app ready to be deployed. There are other folders created in the ./app folder inside the project too. Figure 5-3 shows the folder contents for reference.

Figure 5-3. *Build output folders*

Building from the Command Line

You can build your Android app in two main ways:

- IDEs such as Android Studio and Xamarin have a menu option for building the app once the project is imported.

- Open a shell command and start calling Android build binaries (that are part of the SDK).

■ **Note**   Even the IDE calls into SDK binaries internally, but it is abstracted from the user, hence it seems easier.

Gradle Tasks

The Gradle task that you are interested in here is the one that enables you to build, compile, and output the .apk file. This falls under the category of Gradle tasks viz. build tasks. Figure 5-4 shows the tasks available from the gradle tasks command. Type gradle tasks in the command line and check out the output. It is not necessary to remember all the tasks; however, the more you practice the commands, the easier and faster it gets to script it out.

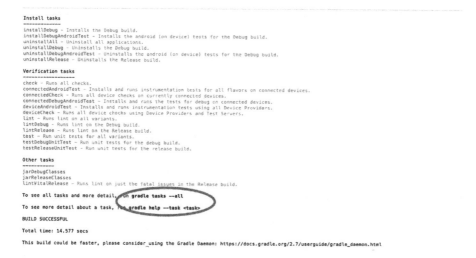

Figure 5-4. Gradle tasks

The Gradle Clean AssembleDebug Task

The assembleDebug gradle task follows the build process, as mentioned in the architecture view, and the clean task cleans the build folder in the project.

Figure 5-5 shows how the process would look when building an app with the following command:

```
gradle clean assembleDebug
```

```
Anyones-Mac-mini:                      pmacharl: gradle clean assembleDebug
:app:clean
:app:preBuild UP-TO-DATE
:app:preDebugBuild UP-TO-DATE
:app:checkDebugManifest
:app:preReleaseBuild UP-TO-DATE
:app:prepareComAndroidSupportAppcompatV72310Library
:app:prepareComAndroidSupportDesign2310Library
:app:prepareComAndroidSupportMultidex101Library
:app:prepareComAndroidSupportRecyclerviewV72310Library
:app:prepareComAndroidSupportSupportV42310Library
:app:prepareComFacebookAndroidFacebookAndroidSdk481Library
:app:prepareComGoogleAndroidGmsPlayServicesBase810Library
:app:prepareComGoogleAndroidGmsPlayServicesBasement810Library
:app:prepareComGoogleAndroidGmsPlayServicesIdentity810Library
:app:prepareComSquareupLeakcanaryLeakcanaryAndroid131Library
:app:prepareComZendeskSdk1411Library
:app:prepareDebugDependencies
:app:compileDebugAidl
:app:compileDebugRenderscript
:app:generateDebugBuildConfig
:app:generateDebugAssets UP-TO-DATE
:app:mergeDebugAssets
:app:generateDebugResValues UP-TO-DATE
:app:generateDebugResources
> Building 63% > :app:mergeDebugResources
```

Figure 5-5. *Gradle clean assembleDebug*

A successful build should look like Figure 5-6.

```
Note: Some input files use or override a deprecated API.
Note: Recompile with -Xlint:deprecation for details.
Note: /Users/pmacharl/gitprojects/hopster_android/app/src/main/java/com/inmar/android/app/hopster/request/p
Note: Recompile with -Xlint:unchecked for details.
:app:compileDebugNdk UP-TO-DATE
:app:compileDebugSources
:app:preDexDebug
:app:dexDebug
:app:validateDebugSigning
:app:packageDebug
:app:zipalignDebug
:app:assembleDebug

BUILD SUCCESSFUL

Total time: 1 mins 59.494 secs
```

Figure 5-6. *assembleDebug is successful*

The .apk File in Debug Mode

The output you are interested in is the .apk file, which is generally found in the relative folder path /app/build/outputs/apk.

The debug app is typically named app-debug.apk and found in the folder structure shown in Figure 5-7.

Figure 5-7. *Apk debug file*

The .apk File in Release Mode

The following command puts the .apk file in app/output/apk/release:

```
./gradlew assembleRelease
```

■ **Note**   To build the app in release mode, you need to sign the app in release mode with keystore and private keys, as detailed at https://developer.android.com/studio/publish/app-signing.html.

71

Building from Android Studio

This section explains how you can build the Android app from Android Studio IDE.

Import the Project

Figure 5-8 shows a sample Android project imported into Android Studio. You would simply click the Play button to build the Android app.

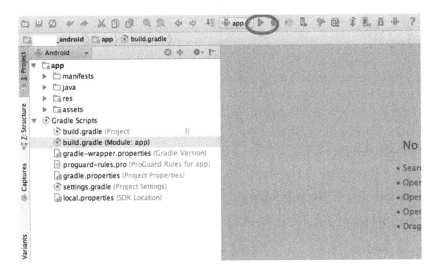

Figure 5-8. *Build the Android app in Android Studio*

The Play button will run the last run configuration. To see a list of all configurations, click the App dropdown, as shown in Figure 5-9. Choose Edit Configurations to see the screen in Figure 5-10.

Figure 5-9. *Edit Configurations in Android Studio*

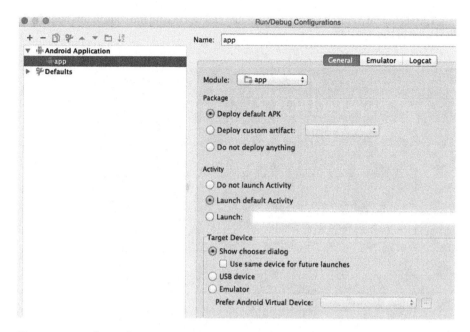

Figure 5-10. *Edit Configuration screen in Android Studio*

Feel free to click each of the tabs and customize as needed. This example uses the defaults.

Android Studio Views

Android Studio provides different views for the project viz.

- Project

- Packages

- Scratches

- Android

- Project files

- Problems

- Production

- Tests

The version of Android Studio that is stable and works with the code in this book is illustrated in Figure 5-11.

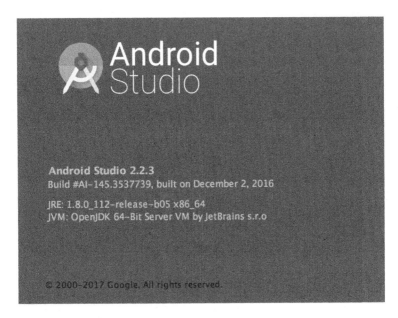

Figure 5-11. *About Android Studio*

Project View

Switch to the Project view so that you can see the changes as Android Studio builds the project. After you run the build configuration, the /app/build/outputs folder and the *.apk file will appear, as shown in Figure 5-12.

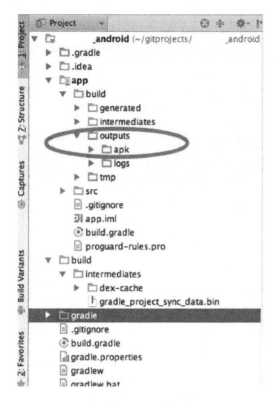

Figure 5-12. *Project view in Android Studio*

■ **Note** Since you configured Android Studio to use the System Gradle and System Android SDK (see the Android system setup section in Chapter 4), the resultant output should be the same as that of running it from the command line in the previous section.

Building the Sample App

This section shows you how to build an app from the source code.

Source Code

This section shows you how to use an app that's already out there and very popular. The Sunshine app is used for tutorials, so let's use it as your candidate.

```
https://github.com/udacity/Sunshine-Version-2
```

Environment

Assuming that you have set up the Android system environment described in Chapter 4, you'll see the environment shown in Figure 5-13.

```
cat /opt/android-sdk-linux/platform-tools/source.properties | grep Pkg.Revision
cat /opt/android-sdk-linux/tools/sources.properties | grep Pkg.Revision
```

```
root@df9305d84dcc:~# cat /opt/android-sdk-linux/platform-tools//source.properties | grep Pkg.Revision
Pkg.Revision=23.1
root@df9305d84dcc:~# cat /opt/android-sdk-linux/tools/source.properties | grep Pkg.Revision
Pkg.Revision=24.4.1
root@df9305d84dcc:~# gradle -v

------------------------------------------------------------
Gradle 2.4
------------------------------------------------------------

Build time:   2015-05-05 08:09:24 UTC
Build number: none
Revision:     5c9c3bc20ca1c281ac7972643f1e2d190f2c943c

Groovy:       2.3.10
Ant:          Apache Ant(TM) version 1.9.4 compiled on April 29 2014
JVM:          1.7.0_80 (Oracle Corporation 24.80-b11)
OS:           Linux 4.1.17-boot2docker amd64
```

Figure 5-13. *Android build environment*

■ **Note**   As mentioned on the git repo, sign up for the weather app key at http://openweathermap.org/appid#use. Once you have the key, place it inside the ~/.gradle/gradle.properties file. If the file doesn't exist, create it.

Clone and Build

To clone and build your sample app, cd into the repo and then run this command:

```
gradle clean assembleDebug
```

■ **Note**   You can see a video of this process at https://vimeo.com/154936765.

Eventually, your successful build should look like Figure 5-14.

```
n edited
:app:processDebugManifest
:app:processDebugResources
:app:generateDebugSources
:app:compileDebugJava
Note: Some input files use or override a deprecated API.
Note: Recompile with -Xlint:deprecation for details.
:app:preDexDebug
:app:dexDebug
:app:processDebugJavaRes UP-TO-DATE
:app:validateDebugSigning
:app:packageDebug
:app:zipalignDebug
:app:assembleDebug

BUILD SUCCESSFUL

Total time: 1 mins 1.511 secs

This build could be faster, please consider using the Gradle Daemon: http://gradle.org/docs/2.4/userguide/gradle_daemon.html
```

Figure 5-14. *The sample app build*

Sample App: app-debug apk

The app-debug.apk sample app is found in the app/build/outputs/apk folder, as shown in Figure 5-15.

```
root@df9305d84dcc:~/Sunshine-Version-2# cd app/build/outputs/apk/
root@df9305d84dcc:~/Sunshine-Version-2/app/build/outputs/apk# ll
total 5856
drwxr-xr-x 2 root root    4096 Feb 10 22:05 ./
drwxr-xr-x 3 root root    4096 Feb 10 22:04 ../
-rw-r--r-- 1 root root 2986111 Feb 10 22:05 app-debug-unaligned.apk
-rw-r--r-- 1 root root 2986491 Feb 10 22:05 app-debug.apk
-rw-r--r-- 1 root root    4704 Feb 10 22:04 manifest-merger-debug-report.txt
root@df9305d84dcc:~/Sunshine-Version-2/app/build/outputs/apk# []
```

Figure 5-15. *Sample app debug apk*

At this point, you can install the debug apk by following the instructions in Chapter 6.

■ **Note**   This source code is used only for demonstrating the build process. Be sure to use your own e-mail ID to create the API key. You need the proper API key to be able to launch the weather app.

77

Connect Android Target

This chapter builds on Chapter 5, in which you learned how to successfully build an .apk file (either through the debug or release APK). Once the .apk file is ready on your filesystem, you have to ensure that you are connected to the target device/emulator where you intend to deploy the .apk file.

Testing with Emulators versus Real Devices

There is lots of information online about when to use emulators versus real devices. After working with mobile apps that utilize Android to the fullest extent, I have come to believe that real-device testing provides significantly higher confidence when releasing the app to production.

You can start your app testing on an emulator, but because emulators cannot fully emulate the hardware, platform, and software conditions, your testing will be incomplete without testing on real devices too.

For emulators, AVD (Android Virtual Device) Manager helps create virtual devices.

For real devices, you have to purchase and maintain them or lease them from device clouds.

© Pradeep Macharla 2017

P. Macharla, *Android Continuous Integration*, DOI 10.1007/978-1-4842-2796-1_6

Using the Android Emulator

The Android Emulator, as the name suggests, emulates an Android device. The utility strives to emulate the mobile hardware components, as well as the gestures (swipe, tap, etc.). You deploy your app into the emulator and then launch and test it as if it were running on a real device.

Features that the emulator cannot imitate are geo-location, actual testing of cell towers, network bandwidth conditions, etc.

For more information about using the Android Emulator, see `https://developer.android.com/studio/run/emulator.html`.

Hardware Acceleration

When launching and configuring AVD, enabling hardware virtualization will greatly improve performance. You can enable this setting by choosing Emulated Performance: Graphics on the Verify Configuration page after you create the AVD.

To enable hardware acceleration, choose GPU Emulation: True when configuring the AVD.

Note that GPU Emulation and Snapshot: Enabled are mutually exclusive.

The URL mentioned previously has more information and details and explains the various configurations possible.

Create a New AVD

After launching the AVD Manager, choose Create Virtual Device to open the screens shown in Figure 6-1.

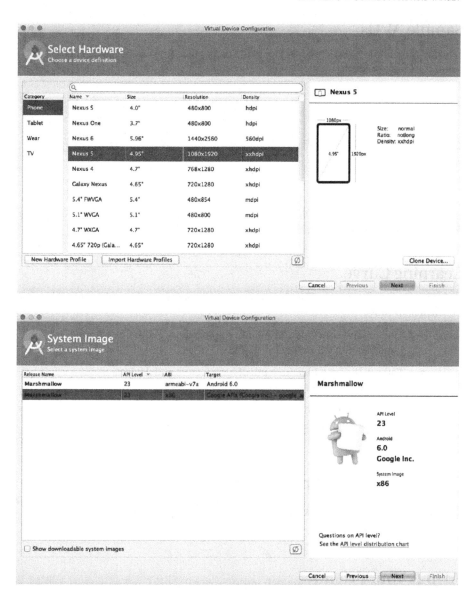

Figure 6-1. *Android Virtual Device*

Sample AVDs

I created the sample AVDs shown in Figure 6-2 on my machine for this book. Feel free to name yours as you see fit.

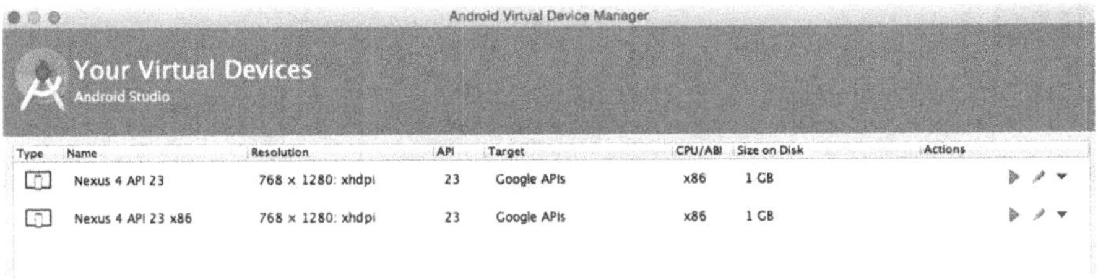

Figure 6-2. *Sample virtual devices*

Learning Curve

In the beginning stages, you should experiment with various combinations of AVDs. This will help you

- Understand concepts and solidify your memory about the various configuration parameters available.

- Fathom the breadth and depth of form factors and devices available in the market.

- Give you context on this knowledge, so that during troubleshooting, you can connect the dots and find the root cause faster.

Connecting the Android Device

This section gets into the details and steps on how to connect an Android device as the target.

ADB Is Your Friend

When connecting real devices to an Android build machine for debugging purposes, ADB (Android Debug Bridge) is your friend. ADB was covered briefly in the "Tools to Know - ADB" section in Chapter 4, and it's explored more in this section.

ADB is a command-line utility included with Google's Android SDK. ADB can control your device over USB from a computer, copy files back and forth, install and uninstall apps, run shell commands, and more.

ADB comes with Android SDK and is available in ANDROID_HOME/platform-tools. You can check it by launching android sdk from the command line. On my machine, as you can see, it is already installed. (I make an assumption here that you have Android SDK installed and configured with PATH variables).

You can verify that the Android SDK platform tools are installed by opening the SDK Manager, as shown in Figure 6-3.

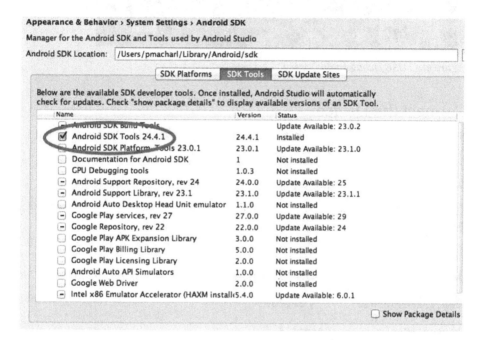

Figure 6-3. *Android SDK Tools*

Enable USB Debug

Before connecting your real device via USB to the computer, you have to enable the Developer options, since only then will ADB be able to talk to this device.

To access these settings, open the Developer options in the system settings. On Android 4.2 and higher, the Developer options screen is hidden by default. To make it visible, go to Settings ➤ About Phone and click Build Number seven times. Return to the previous screen to find the Developer options at the bottom (see Figure 6-4). For more details about this process, see https://developer.android.com/studio/run/device.html.

Your version of the image in Figure 6-4 might differ, depending on your device.

Figure 6-4. *USB Debug enable screen*

Connect the Device

Now you can connect the device using a USB cable to your computer. Open a command prompt (or shell if you are on a Mac) and type:

```
adb devices
```

This command will list all the devices that are connected and have USB debugging enabled.

If all goes well, you should see that your device is recognized, as shown in Figure 6-5.

```
Anyones-Mac-mini:~ pmacharl$ adb devices
List of devices attached
00a219ae09d05912          device

Anyones-Mac-mini:~ pmacharl$
```

Figure 6-5. *adb devices output*

Troubleshooting Tips

Sometimes, you might see unauthorized instead of the device listed, as shown in the following code. The reason this generally happens is because of an improper handshake between the device and the Mac. The RSA fingerprint should be generated and the Mac should have the public key. You should see a pop-up on the device to accept the connection. The effect of unauthorized is that any subsequent commands will throw an error, such as the $ADB_VENDOR_KEYS not being set:

```
pradeep@seleniumframework.com: $ adb devices List of devices attached
209c6111 unauthorized
pradeep@seleniumframework.com: $ adb tcpip 5555 error: device unauthorized
This adbd's $ADB_VENDOR_KEYS is not set; try 'adb kill-server' if that seems
wrong. Otherwise check for a confirmation dialog on your device
```

To solve this unauthorized problem, delete the files adbkey, adbkey.pub from all of these locations. (It is okay to do this, because the files are generated every time the device is connected if one is not found).

`~/.android`

`~/.AndroidStudioXX/.android`

After deleting these files, restart ADB with `adb kill-server` and then `adb start-server`. At this point, you should see a pop-up on the device to accept the connection. Click Yes. For full details of this problem, see `http://forum.xda-developers.com/verizon-lg-g3/help/unable-to-access-adb-t2830087`.

Debugging the WiFi

This section is applicable only if you are interested in exploring with WiFi. As a beginner, a USB wired connection will get you the MVP faster.

It is possible to connect an Android device over WiFi. While the experience is not as smooth as connecting to a USB cable, understanding the fundamentals of networking concepts helps you debug and troubleshoot any connection issues.

I find these two links to be helpful for first timers:

`http://codetheory.in/android-debug-bridge-adb-wireless-debugging-over-wi-fi/`

`https://stackoverflow.com/questions/2604727/how-can-i-connect-to-android-with-adb-over-tcp`

ADB Commands

adb commands are quite helpful in this context.

There are many options for adb. Simply type adb in the command line to see the options. A few I tried were:

`adb get-serialno adb get-devpath`

`adb get-state (prints: offline | bootloader | device) adb usb (back to listening on usb)`

`adb tcp (listen on tcp protocol)`

All these options can also be seen on the command line by typing adb help, as shown in Figure 6-6.

```
adb disable-verity          - disable dm-verity checking on USERDEBUG builds
adb enable-verity           - re-enable dm-verity checking on USERDEBUG builds
adb keygen <file>           - generate adb public/private key. The private key is stored in <file>,
                              and the public key is stored in <file>.pub. Any existing files
                              are overwritten.
adb help                    - show this help message
adb version                 - show version num

scripting:
adb wait-for-device         - block until device is online
adb start-server            - ensure that there is a server running
adb kill-server             - kill the server if it is running
adb get-state               - prints: offline | bootloader | device
adb get-serialno            - prints: <serial-number>
adb get-devpath             - prints: <device-path>
adb remount                 - remounts the /system, /vendor (if present) and /oem (if present) partitions on the
adb reboot [bootloader|recovery]
                            - reboots the device, optionally into the bootloader or recovery program.
adb reboot sideload         - reboots the device into the sideload mode in recovery program (adb root required).
adb reboot sideload-auto-reboot
                            - reboots into the sideload mode, then reboots automatically after the sideload regar
adb reboot-bootloader       - reboots the device into the bootloader
adb root                    - restarts the adbd daemon with root permissions
adb unroot                  - restarts the adbd daemon without root permissions
adb usb                     - restarts the adbd daemon listening on USB
adb tcpip <port>            - restarts the adbd daemon listening on TCP on the specified port
networking:
adb ppp <tty> [parameters]  - Run PPP over USB.
Note: you should not automatically start a PPP connection.
<tty> refers to the tty for PPP stream. Eg. dev:/dev/omap_csmi_tty1
[parameters] - Eg. defaultroute debug dump local notty usepeerdns

adb sync notes: adb sync [ <directory> ]
  <localdir> can be interpreted in several ways:

  - If <directory> is not specified, /system, /vendor (if present), /oem (if present) and /data partitions will be u

  - If it is "system", "vendor", "oem" or "data", only the corresponding partition
    is updated.

environmental variables:
```

Figure 6-6. *ADB help*

Connect Over WiFi

If the mobile device and machine are in the same network (the adb client has to communicate with the adb daemon running on mobile devices), then the experience will be much easier. Ensure that both of them are connected to the same WiFi connection before following these steps.

1. Manually discover the IP address of the device by navigating to Settings ➤ About Phone ➤ Status.

2. Auto discover the IP address with the adb shell.... command. Any devices that have adbd (the adb daemon) listening will show up here. (You can also check if the Android debug interface is enabled on your device by going to Settings ➤ Developer Options ➤ Debugging section ➤ Android Debugging.)

```
C:\Users\pmacharl>adb tcpip 5555

C:\Users\pmacharl>adb devices

List of devices attached
```

```
C:\Users\pmacharl>adb connect 192.168.1.141:5555 connected to
192.168.1.141:5555 C:\Users\pmacharl>adb devices

List of devices attached 192.168.1.141:5555 device

C:\Users\pmacharl>adb shell ip -f inet addr show wlan0

wlan0: <BROADCAST,MULTICAST,UP,LOWER_UP> mtu 1500 qdisc mq state UP qlen
1000 inet 192.168.1.141/24 brd 192.168.1.255 scope global wlan0
C:\Users\pmacharl>adb usb

restarting in USB mode

C:\Users\pmacharl>adb devices

List of devices attached
```

You can also choose to make adb listen on another port, such as 4455.

As you can see in the following code, first the device was connected to the PC/Mac in both USB and TCP/IP (network) mode, hence, there were two rows listed. But when I unplugged the USB cable, only the TCP/IP mode was enabled and hence only one row is shown.

```
C:\Users\pmacharl>adb tcpip 4455

restarting in TCP mode port: 4455

C:\Users\pmacharl>adb shell ip -f inet addr show wlan0

wlan0: <BROADCAST,MULTICAST,UP,LOWER_UP> mtu 1500 qdisc mq state UP qlen
1000 inet 192.168.1.141/24 brd 192.168.1.255 scope global wlan0
C:\Users\pmacharl>adb connect 192.168.1.141:5555 unable to connect to
192.168.1.141:5555 C:\Users\pmacharl>adb connect 192.168.1.141:4455
connected to 192.168.1.141:4455 C:\Users\pmacharl>adb devices

List of devices attached 209c6111 device 192.168.1.141:4455 device

C:\Users\pmacharl>adb devices List of devices attached 192.168.1.141:4455
device
```

Remote Debug Chrome

This section is more useful when you start writing automation scripts and have to identify UI element locators; otherwise, the USB wired connection will help with MVP.

To use remote debugging, you need the following:

- Chrome (version 32) or later installed on your machine

- Android device running Android 4.4+

- USB debugging enabled

- USB cable

Once the basic things are in place, connect your device to the machine using a USB cable. Launch Chrome and open a tab with target `chrome://inspect`. The Chrome screen should resemble Figure 6-7.

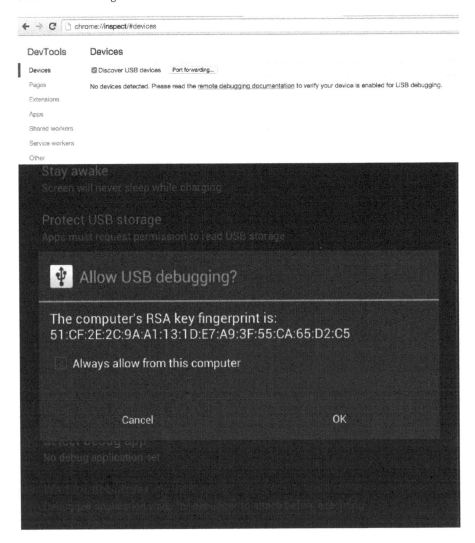

Figure 6-7. Chrome connect

Once you click OK, your device will show up in the browser tab, as shown in Figure 6-8.

Figure 6-8. *Device connected to Chrome*

You can also use the screencast option by clicking the Screencast icon in the upper-right corner of your remote debugging DevTools window. See Figure 6-9.

Figure 6-9. *Screencast option*

CHAPTER 7

Deploy or Install Android App

In Chapters 5 and 6, you learned that the output of the build is the .apk file and the target where you want to install the .apk file has to be connected first. In this chapter, you will learn how to deploy the Android app to the target device that is connected to the Mac.

Connect and Identify the Target

You can identify the emulators or devices that are connected to the machine using these commands:

```
Anyones-mac-mini: pmacharl$ adb devices

List of devices attached

emulator-5554 device
emulator-5556 device
emulator-5558 device
00a219ae09d05912 device
```

Each line after the List of devices attached line represents either an emulator or a device. Emulator has the word emulator-xx prefixed and the device has a serial number.

Direct Commands to Target

adb can direct commands to a specific target using this syntax:

```
adb -s <serial_number> <command>
```

If there is only one device connected, use the -d switch. Similarly, if there is only one emulator connected, use the -e switch.

© Pradeep Macharla 2017
P. Macharla, *Android Continuous Integration*, DOI 10.1007/978-1-4842-2796-1_7

To be on the safe side, using the -s switch will ensure that there is only one matched target.

Install on the Emulator

Install on emulator-5554:

```
adb -s emulator-5556 install myapp.apk
```

Install on Real Device

Install on device:

```
adb -s 00a219ae09d05912 install myapp.apk
```

Command-Line Demonstration

The commands are shown as follows.

```
adb –s <device_id> install app-debug.apk
adb kill-server
adb start-server
adb devices
```

Sometimes, if there is too much delay (more than 5 min), you might have to kill adb and start over again. Most of the time, you don't have to do that, except if you leave the device running for a week or so. That should anyways be handled as part of your mobile device lab set up, where you refresh/reset the adb connections at a certain interval. Figure 7-1 shows the demo.

```
Anyones-Mac-mini:apk pmacharl$ ls -l
total 52608
-rw-r--r--  1 pmacharl  staff  13465517 Dec 20 09:16 app-debug-unaligned.apk
-rw-r--r--  1 pmacharl  staff  13466417 Dec 20 09:16 app-debug.apk
Anyones-Mac-mini:apk pmacharl$ adb devices
List of devices attached
00a219ae09d05912        device

Anyones-Mac-mini:apk pmacharl$ adb -s 00a219ae09d05912 install app-debug.apk
^C
Anyones-Mac-mini:apk pmacharl$ adb -s 00a219ae09d05912 install app-debug.apk
^C
Anyones-Mac-mini:apk pmacharl$ adb kill-server
Anyones-Mac-mini:apk pmacharl$ adb start-server
* daemon not running. starting it now on port 5037 *
* daemon started successfully *
Anyones-Mac-mini:apk pmacharl$ adb devices
List of devices attached
00a219ae09d05912        device

Anyones-Mac-mini:apk pmacharl$ adb -s 00a219ae09d05912 install app-debug.apk
3175 KB/s (13466422 bytes in 4.141s)
        pkg: /data/local/tmp/app-debug.apk
Success
Anyones-Mac-mini:apk pmacharl$ ▌
```

Figure 7-1. *adb commands demo*

Android Studio Demonstration

If you decided to use Android Studio, click the Run button next to the app icon.
The dialog box shown in Figure 7-2 should appear.

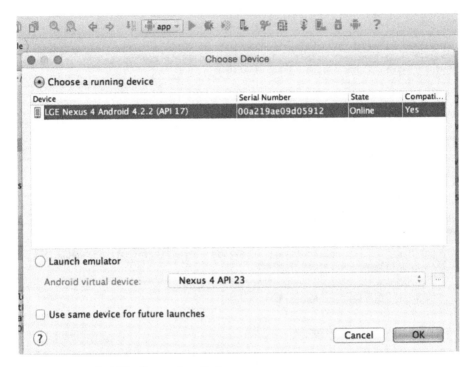

Figure 7-2. *Android Studio app installation*

Click OK. You will be able to see the exact commands in the terminal, as shown in Figure 7-3. Copy the .apk file to the /data/* folder in the device and then install the app. Automatically attach the debugger to the running process and so on. The output should look similar to Figure 7-3. You have plenty of information here to munge, like logcat tab, adb log files, and so on.

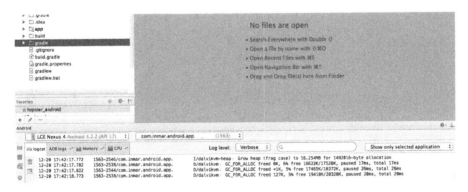

Figure 7-3. *Installation console*

At this point, you should be able to see activity on your mobile device and the app should be launched with the home activity screen displayed.

CHAPTER 8

Working with Appium

This chapter covers more about the Appium tool/framework/ library and explains the what, why and how, so that you will be ready to automate the testing in Chapter 9. For detailed information, you can visit Appium's web site at http://appium.io/.

Why Appium?

This section explains the reasons behind why Appium is my choice for an automated testing platform. You've looked at Appium a little in Chapter 2, and this chapter gets into much more detail.

- **WebDriver JSON wire protocol**: Appium is designed based on the WebDriver protocol, which is set to become a W3C protocol and aligns with the various frameworks that exist with Selenium.

- **Multiple programming languages**: Since WebDriver is HTTP over wire, a WebDriver compatible language can work with Appium. Hence, much like Selenium, Appium client libraries exist for Ruby, Java, Python, PHP, JavaScript, and so on. Even with a newer programming language like Go, you have to implement the contract as defined by WebDriver protocol and it works.

- **Release app vs. Debug app**: While unit testing tests the paths having access to source code, the end user experience has to be tested with a release app build. Appium works on release app builds, which means you'll have relatively greater confidence in integration and end user test automation scenarios.

- **Open source**: Since it is open source, there is a huge community supporting and resolving issues. While some might consider this tough initially, open source with crowd sourcing is the way the software world is moving. It makes sense to invest in such technologies that are flexible and put the decision power in the hands of the developer.

© Pradeep Macharla 2017
P. Macharla, *Android Continuous Integration*, DOI 10.1007/978-1-4842-2796-1_8

Appium Concepts

In the next few sections, you'll learn about the fundamental architectural paradigms on which Appium is built. As you read these sections, you might not be surprised to find a strong correlation between Selenium Web Driver Architecture and Appium (i.e., assuming that you are not just a user of Selenium library, but at some point had to dig deep enough into the Selenium source code or its architecture). It is not a prerequisite to understand this analogy, but it will help you when debugging intricate details. (For example, try capturing the remote IP address of the node on which the test is executing.)

Client/Server Architecture

Appium is at its heart a web server that exposes a REST API. It receives connections from a client, listens for commands, executes those commands on a mobile device, and responds with an HTTP response representing the result of the command execution. The fact that you have a client/server architecture leads to a lot of possibilities. You can write your test code in any language that has a HTTP client API, but it is easier to use one of the Appium client libraries. You can put the server on a different machine than your tests are running on. You can write test code and rely on a cloud services like Sauce Labs to receive and interpret the commands.

Session

Automation is always performed in the context of a session. Clients initiate a session with a server in ways specific to each library, but they all end up sending a `POST /session` request to the server, with a JSON object called the "desired capabilities" object. At this point, the server will start the automation session and respond with a session ID, which is used for sending additional commands.

Desired Capabilities

Desired capabilities are a set of keys and values (i.e., a map or hash) sent to the Appium server to tell it what kind of automation session you're interested in starting up. There are also various capabilities that can modify the behavior of the server during automation. For example, you might set the `platformName` capability to Android to tell Appium that you want an Android session. Or you might set the `chromeAllowPopups` capability to `true` in order to ensure that, during a Safari automation session, you're allowed to use JavaScript to open new windows. See the capabilities document for the complete list of capabilities available for Appium.

Appium Server

Appium is a server written in Node.js. It can be built and installed from source or installed directly from NPM.

Appium Clients

There are client libraries (in Java, Ruby, Python, PHP, JavaScript, and C#) that support Appium's extensions to the WebDriver protocol. When using Appium, you might want to use these client libraries instead of your regular WebDriver client because the community has already implemented most of the calls. You can view the full list of libraries at `https://github.com/appium/appium/blob/master/docs/en/about-appium/appium-clients.md`.

Appium.app and Appium.exe

These GUI wrappers around the Appium server can be downloaded. These come bundled with everything required to run the Appium server, so you don't need to worry about Node. They also come with an Inspector, which enables you to check out the hierarchy of your app. This can come in handy when writing tests.

Appium Design

Appium uses vendor-provided automation frameworks under the hood. That way, you don't need to compile any Appium-specific or third-party code or frameworks in your app. This means you're testing the same app you're shipping. The vendor-provided frameworks are:

- iOS: Apple's UIAutomation

- Android 4.2+: Google's UiAutomator

- Android 2.3+: Google's Instrumentation

Instrumentation support is provided by bundling a separate project, called Selendroid. More information can be found at `appium.io`.

The architecture diagram shown in Figure 8-1 depicts the control flow of the automated test script actions.

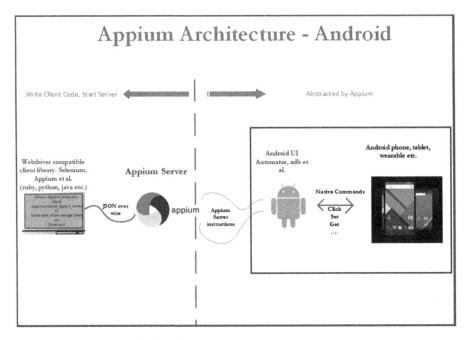

Figure 8-1. *Appium Android architecture*

1. The left side of the blue dotted line is the users' concern.

2. The right side of the blue dotted line is abstracted by Appium.

3. The Appium server talks to the necessary native libraries of Android (adb, UI Automator, etc.) and ensures that the commands are passed to the target device/emulator.

4. adb is part of Android SDK and hence the adb server keeps running inside the device and listens to the commands sent by Appium server.

5. On the host machine that the target device is connected to, adb-server communicates with adbd (adb daemon) on either the emulator or on the real device.

6. The Appium server communicates with the adb server
    through the adb client that comes as part of the Android
    SDK. (None of this is mentioned in the architecture owing to
    granular details.)

7. The Appium server also talks to the UI Automator using its
    internal bootstrap npm module. Prior to Android 4.2, Appium
    used Selendroid to communicate with the UI Automator.
    Hence, when you connect to an Android device that's older
    (i.e., older than the 4.2 SDK), you have to start the Appium
    server by specifying --selendroid-port.

Appium Android

This chapter shows you how to work with a test automation framework that combines
Cucumber, Ruby, and Appium and helps you write automation test cases.

This chapter follows the ATDD (acceptance test driven development) methodology
and hence first writes features and scenarios and subsequently writes the code-behind.

Appium

On the client side, you will use the appium_lib client library and the exposed APIs. It is
also possible to use the Selenium WebDriver and create desired capabilities that specify
Appium as the WebDriver. Having a background on the WebDriver protocol will greatly
help you understand the Appium client library.

Installing the Appium Server

In this section, you install the Appium server and navigate some screens (the default
screens and Android-specific ones).

Download and Install the Appium Server

Follow the instructions on the Appium home page at http://appium.io/. (You can see
that it is a Node.js server, and hence you can start the server from the command line.
However, to keep it simple initially, I just download the .dmg file and double-click to
install and start. Eventually with CI alignment, you will want to go with the Node.js server,
though. Click the Launch button.

GUI Start Android Mode

Figure 8-2 shows Appium Android mode.

Figure 8-2. *Appium Android mode*

Some notes about the Appium server:

- The Appium server is started in Android mode (note that the radio button for Android is checked).

- By default, the Appium server listens on port :4723 on all network interfaces (0.0.0.0).

- It is assumed that you have completed the Android System setup section in Chapter 1 (the Android SDK should be available in the PATH, including its Android tools).

- The Appium server version, as you can see, is 1.4.13.

Appium Server Configuration

Now that you have installed the Appium server, it's time to learn about the configuration options that Appium provides. I do not go into all the options, but instead focus on the ones that matter to the test automation scripts and the debugging context discussed in this book.

Appium Doctor

The mobile environment set up is a little more complex than the web development environment because of the dependencies on various SDKs, emulator/simulators, and their versions. The permutations and combinations increase and there are often questions that come up for an automation engineer in terms of application compatibility. Such questions include:

- What version of Android SDK is running?

- What versions of emulators/simulators are running?

- What mobile devices are attached?

As you can see, setting up a build environment is dependent on how much clarity you have on these questions. You also need to understand any "backward compatibility" vs. "forward compatibility" issues. Unless you are clear about these issues, you are not sure what you are testing. Sure, you can go ahead and test on the developer's environment. But that is not guaranteed to be the same on another developer's machine. Hence, certifying/validating and running the automation tests are heavily dependent on understanding the environment.

For the Appium environment, these settings are necessary and the Appium server can set most of those values. To be precise, it is always advisable to run the Appium Doctor, which does basic checks on the availability of the Android environment. (Clicking the stethoscope icon will run Appium Doctor from the UI.) See Figure 8-3.

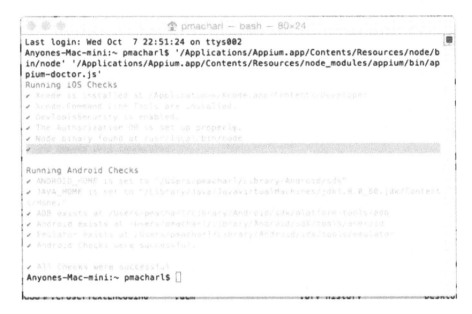

Figure 8-3. *Appium Doctor*

Developer Mode

Because of the many incompatibilities between items in the tuple (such as OS, platform SDKs, Appium server versions, etc.), you should get comfortable playing and installing multiple Appium server versions. The developer mode enables you to use the Appium source, as shown in Figure 8-4.

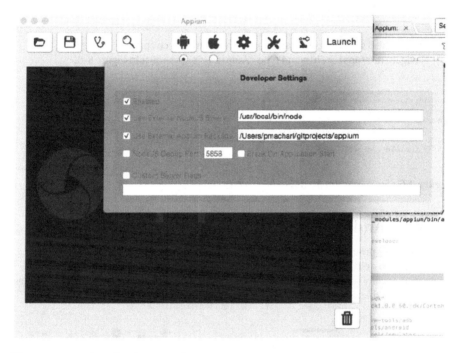

Figure 8-4. *Appium developer mode*

In this case, the Appium source was downloaded to /Users/pmacharl/gitprojects/ appium.

Server Command Line

While GUI is one way to start the Appium server, for CI, you need to be able to start the server from the command line. cmd is also necessary so that you can code away the process of starting the server. It's also important to be able to programmatically (through Bash or PowerShell scripts) kick off the server (such as through a Jenkins CI job).

You can start the command line server by typing `appium`, as shown in Figure 8-5.

```
Anyones-Mac-mini:apk pmacharl$ appium
info: Welcome to Appium v1.4.11 (REV 8cf8311f00e59a2b10fdc1834fcf6d5ace6fbcd0)
info: Appium REST http interface listener started on 0.0.0.0:4723
info: Console LogLevel: debug
info:
info: [debug] Responding to client with success: {"status":0,"value":{"build":{"version":"1.4.11","revision":"8cf8311f00e59a2b10fdc1834fcf6d5ace6fbcd0"}}}
info:     GET /wd/hub/status 200 11.193 ms - 105 {"status":0,"value":{"build":{"version":"1.4.11","revision":"8cf8311f00e59a2b10fdc1834fcf6d5ace6fbcd0"}}}
```

Figure 8-5. *Command line start*

You can also start the command line server from source code.
Navigate to ~/appium/bin and type ./appium.js, as shown in Figure 8-6.

```
Anyones-Mac-mini:bin pmacharl$ pwd
/Users/pmacharl/gitprojects/appium/bin
Anyones-Mac-mini:bin pmacharl$ ./appium.js
info: Welcome to Appium v1.4.13 (REV 88e67ce987d78ce44de252219e07dc176a3511c2)
info: Appium REST http interface listener started on 0.0.0.0:4723
info: Console LogLevel: debug
```

Figure 8-6. *Start Appium from the source code*

Appium Android Settings

Appium server provides many settings for Android. It is beyond the scope of this book to go into each field; however, I want to mention that you can set each of the field values programmatically (which you will see during scripting). Try playing with different settings to get comfortable. See Figure 8-7.

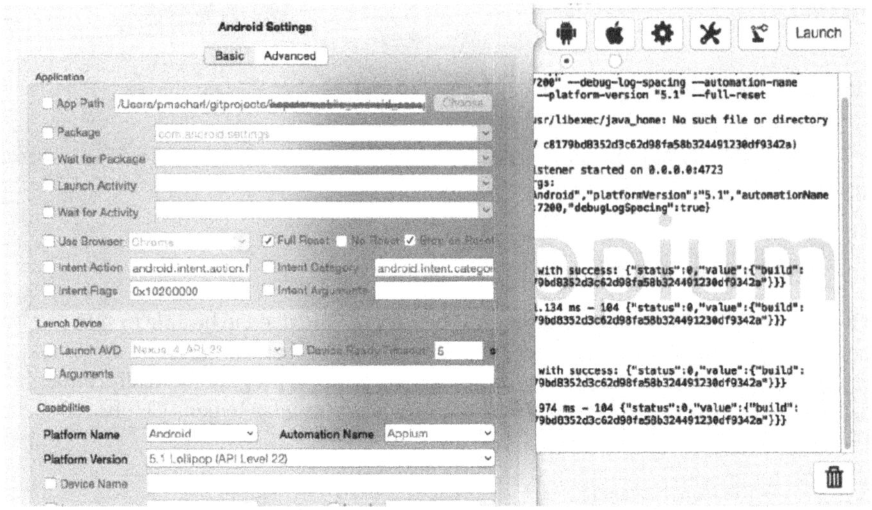

Figure 8-7. *Appium Android settings*

The app path can point to an `.apk` file, for example.

Similarly in Advanced settings, you can point the Android SDK to a specific location instead of the default, which Appium server might look to. This way, you are sure to use only one version of Android SDK and can make updates to that version only. See Figure 8-8.

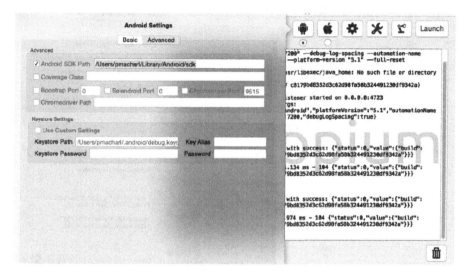

Figure 8-8. *Appium Android Advanced settings*

Appium Server Settings

Finally, the Appium server itself has settings that can be changed, as shown in Figure 8-9.

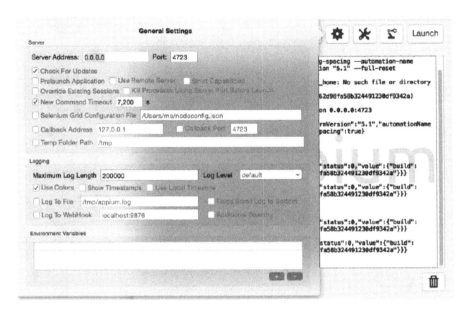

Figure 8-9. *Appium server settings*

■ **Note** All of these settings are also available as server arguments and you can access them by typing `appium -- help` at the command line.

The information you've read at this point might seem overwhelming with respect to the number of options available; however, it will become easier once you start coding away all these complexities. That is one of benefits of CI—it helps automate away mundane and repetitive tasks.

Inspecting an App

Much like how you identify elements of DOM for a web page using Selenium, you follow a similar process for an app. That is, you need to first uniquely identify the locator for an element, before performing an action on it. There are various strategies for that. To get a refresher, check out `http://www.seleniumframework.com/basic-tutorial/html-dom/`.

Most of the UI automation tools and web scrapers have an element identification strategy and knowing it helps you automate actions. It is a good idea to spend some time inspecting your mobile app's "view" as it gets rendered onto the screen. More importantly, understanding the HTML representation and various attributes will help you write automation scripts faster.

This is very similar to using Chrome's dev tools (inspect element), Firefox Inspect Element/Firepath/Firebug, or IE Developer tools. While writing web application automation scripts using Selenium, it is essential that you use these developer tools. Figure 8-10 is an illustration.

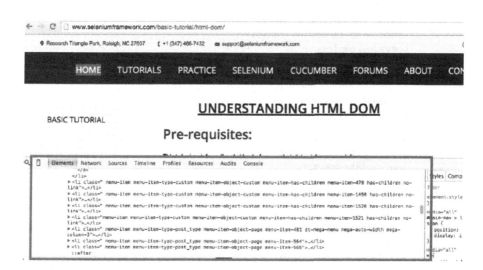

Figure 8-10. *DOM (document object model)*

Appium Ruby Console

The Appium Ruby console (ARC) is a handy tool for quickly looking at the screen HTML. Follow these steps to start using it:

1. Install Ruby 2.0 or higher. Follow the instructions at http://www.seleniumframework.com/basic-tutorial/ setup-ruby-and-components/ if you need help. It is a good idea to have RubyMine IDE installed too, as you will use it in the subsequent chapters.

2. Install arc gems.

```
# Fresh installation
gem uninstall -aIx appium_lib ;\
gem uninstall -aIx appium_console ;\
gem install --no-rdoc --no-ri appium_console bond
```

For troubleshooting instructions, follow this link at
https://github.com/appium/ruby_console.

If you are upgrading, here is what you should expect:

```
Anyones-Mac-mini:~ pmacharl$ pwd
/Users/pmacharl
Anyones-Mac-mini:~ pmacharl$ mkdir arc_tests
Anyones-Mac-mini:~ pmacharl$ cd arc_tests/
Anyones-Mac-mini:arc_tests pmacharl$ arc upgrade
gem uninstall -aIx appium_lib; gem uninstall -aIx
appium_console; gem install --no
-rdoc --no-ri appium_console
Upgrade complete.
```

3. The ARC configuration file. ARC looks for an appium.txt
    file, which has key/value pairs as defined by ARC. There are
    certain key/value pairs expected for Android versus for iOS.
    Here is an example of how you can get started quickly:

```
Anyones-Mac-mini:arc_tests pmacharl$ arc version
appium_console: v1.0.4
appium_lib: v8.0.1
Anyones-Mac-mini:arc_tests pmacharl$ arc setup android
Anyones-Mac-mini:arc_tests pmacharl$ ls
appium.txt
Anyones-Mac-mini:arc_tests pmacharl$ cat appium.txt
[caps]
platformName = "android"
deviceName = "Nexus 7"
app = "./api.apk"
appPackage = "io.appium.android.apis"
appActivity = ".ApiDemos"
[appium_lib]
sauce_username = ""
sauce_access_key = ""
```

- The sauce_username and sauce_access_key can be safely
  ignored until you plan to use Sauce Labs infrastructure for
  execution.

- Access the appPackage and appActivity values for Android
  either by talking to the developer of the app or by using the
  following commands.

Method1

There are two ways to look at the app. The first method executes the following code on the command line:

```
# Returns the package's name, versionCode and so on
aapt dump badging app-debug.apk | grep package:\ name

# Returns all launchable activities. Generally the main entry point to app
will be named as *.MainActivity (but that may change as per developer's
decision) aapt dump badging app-debug.apk | grep launchable-activity
```

Method2

The package name and activity can also be read from the manifest file. You can see the full content of the manifest file by executing the following command. This will output the topology (the metadata and its hierarchy) of your app. The activity that doesn't have any ParentActivity will be the MainActivity in general. The rest of the activities will have ParentActivity. (An activity is a single screen with the user interface.)

```
aapt l -a app-debug.apk
```

■ **Note** The aapt binary is located in the $ANDROID_HOME/build-tools/x.y.z directory.

For full list of appium.txt capabilities (key/value pairs), see https://github.com/appium/appium/blob/master/docs/en/writing-running-appium/caps.md.

■ **Note** On Android, the deviceName capability is currently ignored.

Inspecting Using ARC

Understanding the composition of the application from the UI helps you identify the elements and the operations to be performed on them later. This section looks at the app and identifies the HTML elements.

Prerequisites

Before you start, you need to do the following:

1. Set up an AVD and name it Nexus_4_API_23. The base images are already available with the SDK. See Figure 8-11.

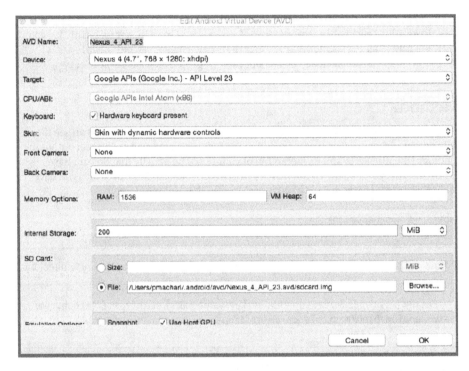

Figure 8-11. *Set up AVD*

2. Notice that Use Host GPU is selected and Snapshot is not. These two fields are mutually exclusive.

3. The Appium server should be running. If not, start it on the default 4723 port.

The Appium.txt File

Using the appium.txt configuration file, type arc in the folder that contains appium.txt:

```
# appium.txt
[caps]
platformName = "Android"
deviceName = "Android"
avd = "Nexus_4_API_23"
app = ""
appPackage = "com.android.settings"
appActivity = ".Settings"
[appium_lib]
sauce_username = ""
sauce_access_key = ""
```

As soon you type arc in the command line, you should see it processing and AVD will be launched. (Patience is a virtue here and AVD's time to launch is based on your machine configuration.)

In the command line, the control returns to ARC (pry), where you can now interact with AVD through appium_lib-provided API calls. See Figure 8-12.

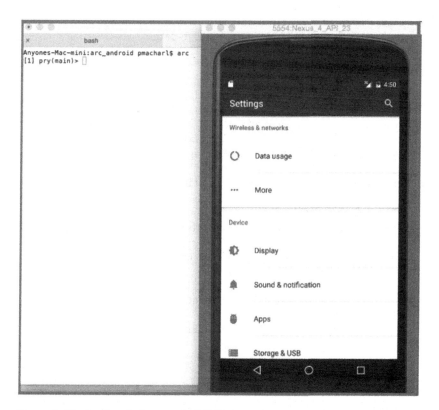

Figure 8-12. *Appium Ruby console (ARC)*

1. The full list of available commands is found at
   https://github.com/appium/ruby_console and is always
   evolving.

2. page_class:

```
Anyones-Mac-mini:arc_android pmacharl$ arc
[1] pry(main)> page_class
22x android.widget.LinearLayout
10x android.widget.FrameLayout
10x android.widget.TextView
6x android.view.View
6x android.widget.RelativeLayout
6x android.widget.ImageView
4x android.view.ViewGroup
1x android.widget.ScrollView
1x hierarchy
```

3. Source:

```
[2] pry(main)> source
<?xml version="1.0" encoding="UTF-8"?>
<hierarchy rotation="0">
<android.widget.FrameLayout index="0" text=""
class="android.widget.FrameLayout"
package="com.android.settings" content-desc=""
checkable="false" checked="false" clickabl
e="false" enabled="true" focusable="false"
focused="false" scrollable="false"
long-clickable="false" password="false"
selected="false" bounds="[0,0][768,1184]"
resource-id="" instance="0">
<android.view.ViewGroup index="0" text=""
class="android.view.ViewGroup" package="
com.android.settings" content-desc=""
checkable="false" checked="false" clickable="false"

[3] pry(main)> id('android:id/decor_content_parent')
#<Selenium::WebDriver::Element:0x323fca632c4ee948 id="1">

[4] pry(main)> id('android:id/decor_content_
parent').methods
[
[ 0] !() Selenium::WebDriver::Element
(BasicObject)
[ 1] !=(arg1) Selenium::WebDriver::Element
(BasicObject)
```

```
[30] pry(main)> xpath('//android.widget.
FrameLayout').get_page_class
"15x android.widget.FrameLayout\n11x android.widget.
LinearLayout\n8x android.widget.
TextView\n6x android.view.View\n6x android.widget.
ImageView\n1x android.widget.GridLayout
\n1x android.widget.ScrollView\n1x android.view.
ViewGroup\n1x android.widget.Relative
Layout\n1x hierarchy"

[31] pry(main)> xpath('//android.widget.
FrameLayout').get_android_inspect
"\nandroid.widget.FrameLayout (1)\n id: com.android.
systemui:id/panel_holder\n\nandroid
.widget.FrameLayout (2)\n"
```

Finally, if you prefer to use the driver object (the Selenium driver) directly instead of using wrapped methods (like d()used previously), you can access the driver object directly.

```
driver.textfields
driver.find_element(:xpath, "//android.widget.FrameLayout")
```

The takeaway from this section is that the more practice and comfort you get with the APIs exposed by Appium, the easier it will be to code the same during scripting.

Using uiautomatorviewer

In the chapter that covers uiautomatorviewer, I introduced the tool. Now let's see how to use it to look at an app.

1. Type uiautomatorviewer in the command line to launch the program ($ANDROID_HOME/platform-tools should be in $PATH).

2. Click the Device Screenshot, uiautomator Dump icon.

3. Select the Android target (avd/device) that uiautomatorviewer should take the XML screenshot from.

4. For AVD, it takes a little bit more time than a real device.

5. After this, you can see the tree hierarchy and use the attributes to further identify elements during automation script writing. See Figure 8-13.

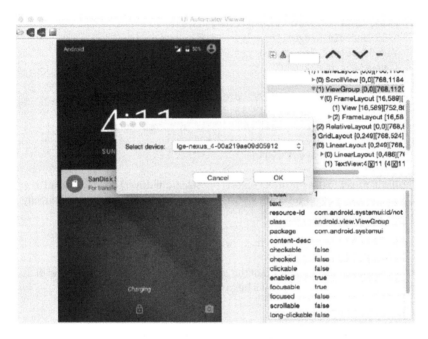

Figure 8-13. *Introspecting on the target device*

In Figure 8-14, you can identify the element that displays the time in Appium using any of the following locator(s):

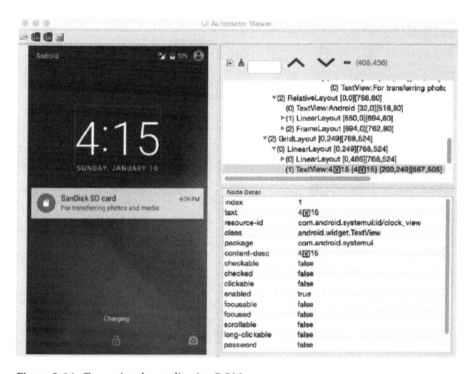

Figure 8-14. *Traversing the application DOM*

```
id('com.android.systemui:id/clock_view')
tag('android.widget.TextView') # Observe that classname is tag in mobile app.
```

CHAPTER 9

Test Strategy and Execution

In the previous chapters, you learned how to build and deploy an app on an Android device.

This chapter covers the details of executing automated tests (written in the Cucumber Gherkin framework) against a target device. This is the final step in getting the full feedback on changes introduced in the app.

Note We are talking about outside-in tests here. Inside-out, i.e. unit, tests involve only a developer. The goal with CI is to get the maximum value as perceived by the end consumer. Hence, the tests mentioned here are integration/end-end tests.

Continuous Test Automation with Cucumber

You can choose any testing framework you like. As an example, I chose Cucumber (with Ruby), because it lets me describe the "what" piece (the features) first. Then I write the "how" layer (the step definitions), i.e. the technical piece, later. In my experience, I feel that this results in good collaboration between multiple roles. If you are a developer and are working in a silo, choose whatever framework fits your needs (JUnit, rspec, testing, et al.). The following links can help you understand the Cucumber basics:

- Why use Cucumber at http://www.seleniumframework.com/cucumber-2/make-a-case/why-cucumber/

- Information about ATDD, BDD, and TDD at http://www.seleniumframework.com/cucumber-2/make-a-case/atdd-tdd-bdd/

- Using continuous test automation at http://www.seleniumframework.com/cucumber-2/make-a-case/continuous-test-automation/

- Learn how Cucumber works at http://www.seleniumframework.com/cucumber-2/make-a-case/how-cucumber-works-2/

© Pradeep Macharla 2017
P. Macharla, *Android Continuous Integration*, DOI 10.1007/978-1-4842-2796-1_9

- Installing Cucumber at `http://www.seleniumframework.com/cucumber-2/install-cucumber/`

- Learn Cucumber's keywords at `http://www.seleniumframework.com/cucumber-2/cucumber-keywords/`

- Step definitions at `http://www.seleniumframework.com/cucumber-2/step-definitions/`

- The basic Ruby tutorial for the web at `http://www.seleniumframework.com/introduction/what-is-ruby/`

I am not going to explain Cucumber and its fundamentals and will assume that you have a basic understanding and have visited these links.

High-Level Mindmap

The high-level explanation of the code you are going to see in the next few sections is as follows:

1. Your Android build process puts the `app-debug.apk` in the `./features/support/resources` folder.

2. Write the Cucumber features.

3. Complete the context code (`env.rb` and `hooks.rb`).

4. List your target devices in `devices.yaml`.

5. List your target emulators in `emulators.yaml`.

6. Define a module that returns the desired capabilities object (representing the device/emulator) to talk to the Appium server.

7. The default Cucumber profile writes HTML and JSON results.

8. Write tests and tag them so that `appPackage` and `appActivity` are defined both for the app to be tested and for the generic settings on the Android device. (The settings needn't be tested in actuality, but we have this example to get started.)

Test Framework

The test framework used here is based on Cucumber, Ruby, and the `Appium_lib` gem. Hence, I describe the "what" in features/scenarios and the "how" in the code-behind (`step_definitions`).

This aligns very well with ATDD (acceptance test-driven development).

Git Repo and Folder Structure

The git repository used for demonstrating test automation in this book can be found at https://github.com/machzqcq/ci_android_acceptancetests.git.

Figure 9-1 shows the folder structure.

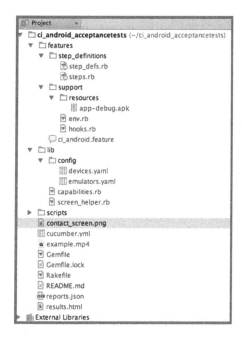

Figure 9-1. *The folder structure*

- ci_android_acceptancetests is the Cucumber project root.

- The features folder contains features.

- The step_definitions folder contains the code-behind. In this case, it has two Ruby files. There can be any number and can be spread across files.

- The support folder is the standard Cucumber support folder, i.e., the code in this folder is executed when the Cucumber process starts and the resources folder contains app-debug.apk, which is the output of the build process.

- env.rb is usually the file where modules for the Cucumber project and any other context must be loaded.

- hooks.rb contains the pre- and post-conditions for scenarios. You can put this in env.rb instead, but by convention, I use hooks.

- `ci_android.feature` contains the scenarios or tests.

- The `lib` folder is defined by this framework to store the code that is mixed in. It also contains configuration definitions for devices and emulators.

- `devices.yaml` contains device definitions.

- `emulators.yaml` contains emulator definitions.

- `capabilities.rb` contains the module that returns the desired capabilities object.

- The `screen_helper.rb` module is for future use to apply page object patterns.

- The `scripts` folder is to quickly test something before you formalize it in features. It's not necessary, but it's helpful for writing quick snippets of code.

- `contact_screen.png` was a screenshot taken by one of the scenarios.

- `cucumber.yml` is the configuration file for Cucumber.

- `example.mp4` is the screen capture taken when executing the scenario. (See the adb tutorial section on how to take a screen recording).

- `Gemfile` contains the gems used in this project.

- `Gemfile.lock` is created when you run `bundle install`.

- `Rakefile` is not used at this point, although you can define higher-level tasks.

- `README.md` contains the readme file for this project.

- `reports.json` is the JSON-formatted output of Cucumber.

- `reports.html` is the HTML-formatted output of Cucumber.

Writing the Tests

This section shows you how to write a couple of Cucumber scenarios. Since it is simple English, the scenarios don't need extra explanation.

Cucumber Scenarios (ci_android.feature)

First consider the Cucumber scenario (see Figure 9-2).

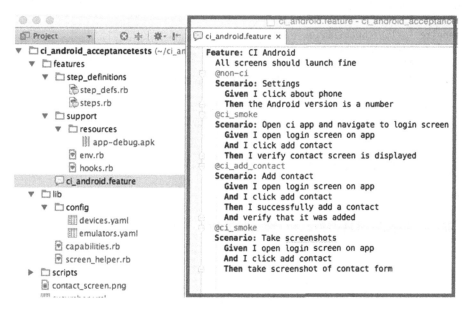

Figure 9-2. *Feature file location in the folder structure*

```
Feature: CI Android
All screens should launch fine
@non-ci
Scenario: Settings
    Given I click about phone
    Then the Android version is a number
@ci_smoke
Scenario: Open ci app and navigate to login screen
    Given I open login screen on app
    And I click add contact
    Then I verify contact screen is displayed
@ci_add_contact
Scenario: Add contact
    Given I open login screen on app
    And I click add contact
    Then I successfully add a contact
    And verify that it was added
@ci_smoke
Scenario: Take screenshots
    Given I open login screen on app
    And I click add contact
    Then take screenshot of contact form
```

hooks.rb

The values for appActivity and appPackage were retrieved using the aapt command, as described in Chapter 8.

```
require './lib/capabilities'
include DesiredCapabilities
Before('@ci_smoke') do
caps = local_capabilities(app='app-debug.apk',appActivity='com.example.
android.conta
ctmanager.ContactManager',
appPackage='com.example.android.contactmanager')
@driver = Appium::Driver.new(caps)
Appium.promote_appium_methods AppiumWorld
puts "Execute anything before scenario/test case"
@driver.start_driver
end
Before('@ci_add_contact') do
caps = local_capabilities(app='app-debug.apk',appActivity='com.example.
android.conta
ctmanager.ContactManager',
appPackage='com.example.android.contactmanager')
@driver= Appium::Driver.new(caps)
Appium.promote_appium_methods AppiumWorld
puts "Execute anything before scenario/test case"
@driver.start_driver
end
Before('@non-ci') do
caps = local_capabilities(app='',appActivity='.Settings',appPackage='com.
android.set
tings')
@driver = Appium::Driver.new(caps)
Appium.promote_appium_methods AppiumWorld
puts "Execute anything before scenario/test case"
@driver.start_driver
end
After do |scenario|
if scenario.failed?
@driver.screenshot("#{scenario.name}_failed.png")
end
@driver.driver_quit
puts "Execute anything after scenario/test case"
end
```

env.rb

As you can see, you create a custom World class, which is used in hooks.rb.

```
require 'rspec/expectations'
require 'appium_lib'
require 'cucumber/ast'
require 'yaml'
require 'active_support/core_ext/hash'
# Create a custom World class so we don't pollute `Object` with Appium
methods
class AppiumWorld
end
World do
AppiumWorld.new
end
$devices = YAML.load(File.open('./lib/config/devices.yaml'))
$emulators = YAML.load(File.open('./lib/config/emulators.yaml'))
```

Devices Lab

My device lab is shown in Figure 9-3. At this point, there are only three devices; however, you can connect many more by purchasing an USB extension cord.

Figure 9-3. *Mini device lab*

You need to start the Appium server(s) on the available network ports to talk to each of these devices. For this example, I execute on only one device.

devices.yaml

You define the devices configuration in a YAML file, as shown in the following code. If you have a new device to be connected, copy and paste the block and then replace the values (serial, name, and port) as needed.

Ensure that you provide a different port for each device.

■ **Note** This port should be the same value that the Appium server starts on (the default Appium server port is 4723).

```
devices:
huawei-nexus_6p-84B5T15A17000142:
caps:
platformName : Android
deviceName : huawei-nexus_6p-84B5T15A17000142
app: app-debug.apk
appActivity : .Settings
appPackage : com.android.settings
appium_lib:
sauce_username:
sauce_access_key:
port: 4768
motorola-google-ZX1B222FCD:
caps:
platformName : Android
deviceName : motorola-google-ZX1B222FCD
app: app-debug.apk
appActivity : .Settings
appPackage : com.android.settings
appium_lib:
sauce_username:
sauce_access_key:
port: 4778
```

emulators.yaml

Similar to the devices, you must also define the emulators' configuration. You should have already defined the AVDs by this time. See the AVD Manager to learn how to add AVDs.

```
emulators:
Nexus_5_API_23_x86:
caps:
platformName : Android
deviceName : IGNORED
avd : Nexus_5_API_23_x86
app: app-debug.apk
appActivity : .Settings
appPackage : com.android.settings
appium_lib:
sauce_username:
sauce_access_key:
Nexus_4_API_23_x86:
caps:
platformName : Android
deviceName : IGNORED
avd: Nexus_4_API_23
app: app.debug.apk
appActivity : .Settings
appPackage : com.android.settings
appium_lib:
sauce_username:
sauce_access_key:
```

Capabilities.rb

This file returns the desired capabilities object and is mixed in hooks.rb:

```
module DesiredCapabilities
def local_capabilities(app={},appActivity={},appPackage={})
if ENV['DEVICE'].nil? and ENV['EMULATOR'].nil?
puts "One of the targets DEVICE or EMULATOR has to be set"
puts "Allowed devices: #{$devices['devices'].keys}"
puts "Allowed emulators: #{$emulators['emulators'].keys}"
exit
end
if ENV['DEVICE'].nil? || ENV['DEVICE'].empty?
puts "Did not specify device target. Assuming emulator is set"
caps = $emulators['emulators']["#{ENV['EMULATOR']}"]
if app.nil? || app.empty?
caps['caps'] = caps['caps'].except('app')
```

```
else
caps['caps']['app'] = File.join(Dir.pwd,"features/support/resources", app)
end
caps['caps']['appActivity'] = appActivity
caps['caps']['appPackage'] = appPackage
end
if ENV['EMULATOR'].nil? || ENV['EMULATOR'].empty?
puts "Did not specify emulator target. Assuming device is set"
caps = $devices['devices']["#{ENV['DEVICE']}"]
if app.nil? || app.empty?
caps['caps'] = caps['caps'].except('app')
else
caps['caps']['app'] = File.join(Dir.pwd,"features/support/resources", app)
end
caps['caps']['appActivity'] = appActivity
caps['caps']['appPackage'] = appPackage
end
caps
end
end
```

ScreenHelper.rb (Not Used)

Page object framework enthusiasts can use this module to define page objects using page-factory.

```
module ScreenHelper
def visit(page_class, &block)
on page_class, true, &block
end
def on(page_class, visit=false, &block)
page_class = class_from_string(page_class) if page_class.is_a? String
page = page_class.new @browser, visit
block.call page if block
page
end
def wait_for_ajax(timeout = 10)
timeout.times do
return true if browser.execute_script('return jQuery.active').to_i == 0
sleep(1)
end
raise Watir::Wait::TimeoutError, "Timeout of #{timeout} seconds exceeded on
wait
ing for Ajax."
end
private
def class_from_string(str)
```

```
str.split('::').inject(Object) do |mod, class_name|
mod.const_get(class_name)
end
end
end
```

Step Definitions

Here are the step definitions:

```
Given /^I click about phone$/ do
scroll_to('About phone').click
end
Given /^the Android version is a number$/ do
android_version = 'Android version'
scroll_to android_version
view = 'android.widget.TextView'
version = xpath(%Q(//#{view}[preceding-sibling::#{view}[@text="#{android_
version}"]]
)).text
if !version.match(/\w/).nil? || !version.match(/\d/).nil?
puts "Version: #{version} pass"
else
puts "Version: #{version} is NOT a word or number"
# valid = !version.match(/\d/).nil?
end
# expect(valid).to eq(true)
end
```

Now step_defs.rb:

```
Given(/^I open login screen on app$/) do
add_contact = id('com.example.android.contactmanager:id/addContactButton')
exists(post_check=30) { add_contact.text == 'Add Contact' } ? puts('Add
Contact exists') : puts('App failed to open')
end
And(/^I click add contact$/) do
id('com.example.android.contactmanager:id/addContactButton').click
end
Then(/^I verify contact screen is displayed$/) do
expect(id('android:id/text1').text).to eql("seleniumfrmwrkguest@gmail.com")
end
Then(/^I successfully add a contact$/) do
id('com.example.android.contactmanager:id/contactNameEditText').type "blah"
id('com.example.android.contactmanager:id/contactPhoneEditText').type "123-
456-7890"
```

```
id('com.example.android.contactmanager:id/contactPhoneTypeSpinner').click
tags('android.widget.CheckedTextView')[2].click
id('com.example.android.contactmanager:id/contactEmailEditText').type
"pradeep@seleniumframework.com"
id('com.example.android.contactmanager:id/contactSaveButton').click
end
And(/^verify that it was added$/) do
expect(id('com.example.android.contactmanager:id/contactEntryText').text).
to eql('blah')
end
Then(/^take screenshot of contact form$/) do
@driver.screenshot("contact_screen.png")
end
```

Explanation of Key Concepts

This section explains the key concepts.

- The locators are retrieved through `uiautomator` or `arc` or by printing the source. See the section entitled "Introspecting App" to learn about retrieving locators.

- In the step definitions, you must identify the elements, then retrieve the text and assert it against the expected text.

- You also need to perform actions like clicking and setting text by filling in the contact form and verifying that the contact was saved,

- It is also possible to take a screenshot at any point by calling the method on the driver object.

Executing the Test from the Local Lab

Now that you have written your tests, you can execute them. These examples assume that you connected your devices through USB or WiFi.

Start the Appium Server

To start the Appium server, follow these steps:

1. Identify the device using adb devices. (You should have connected the device either through USB or WiFi).

2. Start the Appium server on the port (the same port that was defined for the device in the devices.yaml file) and specify the bootstrap port (must be at least 10 ports apart).

```
Anyones-Mac-mini:~ pmacharl$ adb devices
List of devices attached
ZX1B222FCD device
Anyones-Mac-mini:~ pmacharl$ appium -p 4778 -bp 4789 -U ZX1B222FCD
info: Welcome to Appium v1.4.11 (REV
8cf8311f00e59a2b10fde1834fcf6d5ace6fbcd0)
info: Appium REST http interface listener started on 0.0.0.0:4778
info: [debug] Non-default server args: {"udid":"ZX1B222FCD","port":4778,
"bootstrapPort":4789}
info: Console LogLevel: debug
```

Execute the Test

The DEVICE or EMULATOR parameters are mandatory since a target is required to run the test. If none is specified, a validation error is raised. The permissible values are the keys inside the devices.yaml/emulators.yaml file.

- Example 1: DEVICE=motorola-google-ZX1B222FCD

- Example 2: EMULATOR=Nexus_4_API_23_x86

Execute settings scenario on a device:

```
bundle exec cucumber features/ci_android.feature:5 DEVICE=motorola-google-
ZX1B222FCD
```

Execute open login screen:

```
bundle exec cucumber features/ci_android.feature:9 DEVICE=motorola-google-
ZX1B222FCD
```

Add contact scenario:

```
bundle exec cucumber features/ci_android.feature:15 DEVICE=motorola-google-
ZX1B222FCD
```

Take screenshot scenario:

```
bundle exec cucumber features/ci_android.feature:21 DEVICE=motorola-google-
ZX1B222FCD
```

Figure 9-4 shows the execution alongside the code.

Figure 9-4. *Execution alongside code*

To see a full video of the execution, visit `https://www.youtube.com/watch?v=In9sCFrv-D0&feature=youtu.be`.

The device screen is exported and you can see the server and target execution in one screen. That is one of the challenges in demonstrating the automation value on the mobile side. For the web, since the browser launches on the machine itself, it is relatively easier.

Executing the Test from Sauce Labs

As you continue executing tests and attempt to increase the coverage on various devices, form factors become a critical issue. Sure, you can keep buying devices; however, there is not much economy of scale in doing so. Wouldn't it be nice to have that non-core competency of maintaining the devices offloaded to a service provider?

Sure enough, there are many providers out there that do just that, including Sauce Labs, Perfecto Mobile, and ExperiTest. This chapter provides an example of Sauce Labs, because they are aligned with Appium.

What Is Sauce Labs?

Sauce Labs provides both infrastructure and platform cloud services.

- **Infrastructure:** Over 700 combinations of browsers and OS platforms. Includes mobile emulators and simulators, as well as real devices.

- **Platform:** Selenium Grid platform, so that automation tests that talk in the WebDriver protocol can execute tests against the underlying infrastructure.

- **User Interface:** A nice GUI for manual testing and on-demand availability of browsers, emulators, simulators, and real mobile devices. Sauce Labs' features cannot be summed up here, but I encourage you to read more about it online.

Running Against Sauce Labs

You can run Sauce Labs on real devices or emulators.

Running on Real Devices

Upload your app to the Sauce storage. Replace the values with your Sauce credentials:

```
$ curl -u $SAUCE_USERNAME:$SAUCE_ACCESS_KEY -X POST "http://saucelabs.com/
rest/v1/stor age/$SAUCE_USERNAME/my_app.zip?overwrite=true" -H "Content-
Type: application/octet-str eam" -data-binary @my_app.zip
```

Now add the real device configuration in devices.yaml. An example is shown in Figure 9-5.

Figure 9-5. Sauce Labs configuration in devices.yaml

Feature Files (ci_android.feature)

Here is the feature file:

```
@ci_add_contact_sauce
Scenario: Contact on sauce
        Given I open login screen on app
        And I click add contact
        Then I successfully add a contact
```

Hooks.rb File

Here is the Hooks.rb file:

```
Before('@ci_add_contact_sauce') do

  caps = sauce_capabilities(app='http://saucelabs.com/example_files/app-
debug.apk',app
Activity='com.example.android.contactmanager.ContactManager',
appPackage='com.example.android.contactmanager')

  @driver= Appium::Driver.new(caps)
  Appium.promote_appium_methods AppiumWorld
  puts "Execute anything before scenario/test case"
  @driver.start_driver
end
```

Execute the File

Now run it:

```
bundle exec cucumber features/ci_android.feature:26 DEVICE=saucelabs_
samsung_galaxy_s4
```

Feedback

Once you kick off the execution, you should instantly see a row on the Sauce dashboard that represents the execution session. See Figure 9-6.

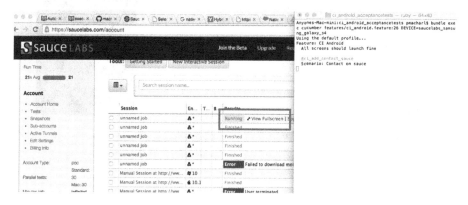

Figure 9-6. *The Sauce Labs console*

When the execution is complete, the results should look like Figure 9-7.

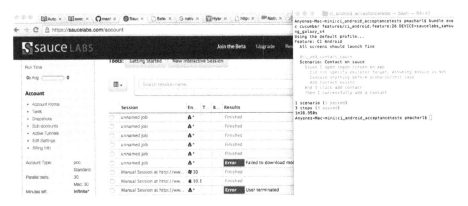

Figure 9-7. *Sauce Labs execution results*

Clicking the execution session row, you can find information that will help you analyze the results (including videos, Appium logs, screenshots, and detailed logs). Figure 9-8 shows the Sauce Labs execution video.

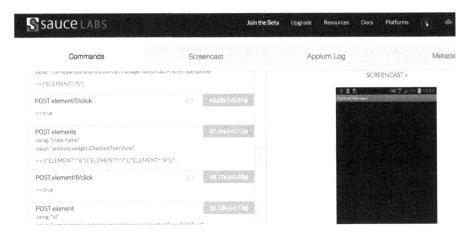

Figure 9-8. *Sauce Labs execution video*

The results can also be found in the `results.html` file in the root folder (see Figure 9-9), since the example outputs the HTML results as specified in the `cucumber.yaml` configuration file.

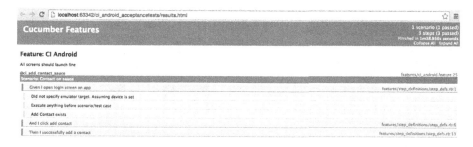

Figure 9-9. *Cucumber results*

Running on Emulators

Since Sauce Labs provides emulators, the difference is the way you construct the desired capabilities object, and therefore replace the values in `emulators.yaml`. The values can be read from their documentation, found at `https://wiki.saucelabs.com/display/DOCS/Platform+Configurator#/`.

Parallel Devices Automation

This section contains a brief description on how to execute tests in parallel across devices.

Executing automated tests in parallel is dependent on any of the following (see Figure 9-10):

- App support of parallel sessions

- Whether the test automation framework can initiate parallel tests

- Whether there are multiple Appium servers, one for each device, with dedicated ports

135

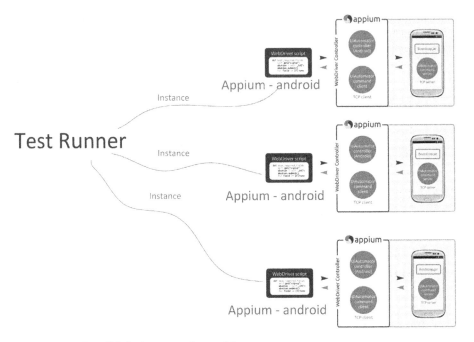

Figure 9-10. *Parallel devices execution architecture*

Parallel execution also might result in race conditions, so understanding the application domain and call path is extremely important before you can certify parallel tests.

Start Appium Servers on Different Ports

Here is the command to start multiple Appium servers. Be sure to open a new shell for each of these Appium servers.

```
appium -p 4724 -bp 4726 -U EGxxxxxxxxx
appium -p 4734 -bp 4736 -U EGxxxxxxxxx
```

If your target device/emulator has an SDK less than 4.2 or an API level less than 16, Appium uses `selendroid`. In that case, you have to append `--selendroid-port` to the previous command (generally stay 10 ports apart, because Appium uses +1 port of `-p`):

```
appium -p 4724 -bp 4726 --selendroid-port 4737 -U EGxxxxxxxxx
appium -p 4734 -bp 4736 --selendroid-port 4747 -U EGxxxxxxxxx
```

If you are running Appium from the `Appium.exe` path, then use:

```
node appium --nodeconfig path\to\nodeconfig.json -p 4724 -bp 5724
```

Or if you're using cmd, use this command:

```
appium --nodeconfig path\to\nodeconfig1.json -p 4724 -bp 5724
```

Client Side

This refers to the test automation framework code that can connect to the Appium servers. You must write logic to instantiate the driver session based on the available pool of devices/emulators. In this case, you have to parse the devices.yaml or emulators.yaml file and create a $driver session by connecting to the corresponding port.

Index

▪ A, B

Acceptance test driven development (ATDD), 99
Amazon Device Lab, 22
Android app
  deploying/installing, 9
  installation process, 5
    CI tool stack, 8
    Jenkins, 5–6
    Nexus, 6–7
    SonarQube, 7
  Mac environment, 4
  mobile devices, 4
  network, 4
  platform, 5
  testing (automating), 9–10
  Windows *vs.* Mac, 3
Android app build process, 9, 67
  Android Studio, 72
    importing the project, 72–73
    project view, 74–75
    views, 73–74
  command line, 69
    .apk file in debug mode, 71
    .apk file in release mode, 71
    Gradle clean assembleDebug task, 70
    Gradle tasks, 69
  output, 68
  overview, 67
  perspective on, 68
  sample app, 75
    app-debug apk, 77
    clone and build, 76
    environment, 76
    source code, 75

Android Debug Bridge (ADB), 60, 82–83
Android device, 82
  ADB, 82–83
  connecting the device, 84
  enable USB debug, 83–84
  troubleshooting tips, 84–85
Android Emulator, 80
  creating new AVD, 80–81
  hardware acceleration, 80
  learning curve, 82
  sample AVDs, 82
Android Espresso, 17
Android SDK, 49
  quick checks, 51–52
  standalone SDK, 50–51
  tools, 59
    ADB, 60
    Android Device Monitor, 65
    AVD Manager, 62–63
    record video, 60
    SDK Manager, 63–64
    uiautomatorviewer, 61–62
Android Studio, 52
  associate system SDK, 54–55
  basics, 53–54
  demonstration, 93–94
  with Gradle, 57–58
Android virtual device (AVD)
  Manager, 79
Appium, 17, 95
  app, inspecting, 106–107
  ARC, 107–109
  ARC, inspecting using, 109–113
  concepts, 96
    Android, 99
    Appium.app and Appium.exe, 97

Get the eBook for only $5!

Why limit yourself?

With most of our titles available in both PDF and ePUB format, you can access your content wherever and however you wish—on your PC, phone, tablet, or reader.

Since you've purchased this print book, we are happy to offer you the eBook for just $5.

To learn more, go to http://www.apress.com/companion or contact support@apress.com.

Apress®